naked
imperfection

a memoir

gillian deacon

PENGUIN

an imprint of Penguin Canada Books Inc., a Penguin Random House Company

Published by the Penguin Group

Penguin Canada Books Inc., 90 Eglinton Avenue East, Suite 700,
Toronto, Ontario, Canada M4P 2Y3

Penguin Group (USA) LLC, 375 Hudson Street, New York, New York 10014, U.S.A.
Penguin Books Ltd, 80 Strand, London WC2R 0RL, England
Penguin Ireland, 25 St Stephen's Green, Dublin 2, Ireland (a division of Penguin Books Ltd)
Penguin Group (Australia), 707 Collins Street, Melbourne, Victoria 3008, Australia
(a division of Pearson Australia Group Pty Ltd)
Penguin Books India Pvt Ltd, 11 Community Centre, Panchsheel Park, New Delhi – 110 017, India
Penguin Group (NZ), 67 Apollo Drive, Rosedale, Auckland 0632, New Zealand
(a division of Pearson New Zealand Ltd)
Penguin Books (South Africa) (Pty) Ltd, 24 Sturdee Avenue, Rosebank, Johannesburg 2196,
South Africa

Penguin Books Ltd, Registered Offices: 80 Strand, London WC2R 0RL, England

First published 2014

1 2 3 4 5 6 7 8 9 10 (WEB)

Manufactured in Canada

LIBRARY AND ARCHIVES CANADA CATALOGUING IN PUBLICATION

Deacon, Gillian, author,
Naked imperfection : a memoir / Gillian Deacon.

ISBN 978-0-14-318851-3 (pbk.)

1. Deacon, Gillian. 2. Women broadcasters—Canada—Biography. 3. Women environmentalists—
Canada—Biography. 4. Women authors, Canadian (English)—Biography. 5. Breast—Cancer—
Patients—Canada—Biography. 6. Perfectionism (Personality trait). I. Title.

PN1990.72.D32A3 2014   384.54092   C2013-904282-2

eBook ISBN 978-0-14-319192-6

Visit the Penguin Canada website at **www.penguin.ca**

Special and corporate bulk purchase rates available; please see
www.penguin.ca/corporatesales or call 1-800-810-3104, ext. 2477.

for grant, the rock.
and for deb, the angel.

Cancer connects us to one another because having cancer is an embodiment of the existential paradox that we all experience: we feel that we are immortal, yet we know that we will die.

—Alice Stewart Trillin, "Of Dragons and Garden Peas," *New England Journal of Medicine*, 1981

Ring the bells that still can ring
Forget your perfect offering
There is a crack in everything
That's how the light gets in.

—Leonard Cohen, "Anthem"

my mother begins
most days with a list

PENNED IN HER TIDY, looping hand, often on the back of a used envelope or a section of pulpy grey cardboard cut from a cereal box bound for the recycling bin, her list lays out the stepping stones of a master plan for the day ahead: appointments, tasks, calls to place, errands to run. Or for the meal ahead: multiple courses, laid out in mouth-watering detail, along with sidebar lists of ingredients to purchase and schedules for timely assembly.

A plan, it seemed to my watchful young eye, shows us the way forward, lights the path. A plan helps us be prepared and efficient. Without a plan, we are lost—or worse, drifting.

Though it was never committed to paper in list form, I had a master plan. It went something like this: Get a job that made a difference. Marry a man who made a difference. Have some kids who would grow up to make a difference. And save the planet in the process. And I almost pulled it off. There have been many jobs; in each one I chipped away like a warbler at suet, pecking at the monumental need for health and environmental education, connecting readers and television audiences to their own relationship with the natural world. There has been just one husband, whose bottomless

1

commitment to social reform and environmental activism is matched only by his generous heart and dazzling creativity. There are three children, who melt my heart anew each day with their sturdy courage, sunny attitudes, and fiery passion for what they know is right. And then there was the cancer diagnosis. The point at which the compulsion to redress every planetary wrong fell away. The incident that yanked me out of the reverie of a tidier future and thrust me into the unambitious and naked imperfection of right now.

dented cup

A WOMAN I DON'T RECOGNIZE approaches me at the party. She wears her blond hair braided into coils on the top of her head like a Swiss milkmaid. She looks like her name should be Heidi. "Hi, Gill? I wanted to say hello. My name's Heidi." She explains that she was an assistant editor at the women's magazine where I had written a monthly Green-Your-Life column before I got cancer, featuring chirpy friendly tips for the woman who wants to have it all and save the earth while she's at it. We had emailed a few exchanges over editing points, but never met. "I just had to come over and see how you were doing, after being sick. How are you feeling? I was so stunned to hear what had happened to you." Heidi is thin and pretty, her skin is like springtime. Her hands look too delicate to haul milk pails up the Alps. She touches my forearm with her long, gentle fingers. "It's just that you were so *perfect*. I always thought that I wasn't doing enough compared to you, for the planet and for my health. I mean it just didn't make sense to me that you could get sick. It still doesn't!" She shakes her head a little, lifts her hand from my arm and pitches it upwards, a gesture of befuddlement.

A roar of laughter erupts from across the room; beside me, a woman in a red and white sweater bites into a flaky canapé, balances her drink awkwardly as she wipes the corners of her mouth with a paper napkin. The other party guests are, naturally, oblivious to our conversation. Instinctively I wanted someone to hear this exchange, to witness this transaction, the bestowing, from one woman to another, of the much-coveted laurel of perfection. But no one else heard.

There it was, the label I'd worked so long and hard to deserve. *Perfect.* Everything under control. But instead of feeling like a reward for all the health- and earth-minded sacrifices I'd made, the very notion of impeccability seemed ridiculous. Hearing it that day, over the din of cocktail chatter, the word sounded tinny and hollow, a dented pewter cup posing as gilded chalice. Her words told me two things: first, that my performance as an accomplished environmental journalist who had all the answers for how to save the world and myself along with it had fooled Heidi as well as me; second, that whatever delusions she held about my impenetrability had passed. I smiled, enjoying the camaraderie of the uncertain.

born first

THE LIVING ROOM in my childhood home was proper—the kind of space a child entered cautiously, never when carrying food or art supplies. Behind the floral chintz chesterfield (my mother said *couch* was a word to describe basement furniture), a large picture window looked out onto the front yard, bordered by a willow tree on the right and a large jack pine on the left, just beside the driveway. I mostly remember the view out that window being about a dozen different shades of green. Kimbark Boulevard had no sidewalks; like all roads in the North Toronto neighbourhood where I grew up, it simply petered out into light gravel that eventually ran into the grass of each front yard. Painted white rocks bordered the house on the opposite corner from ours, a decorative trim stitched along its periphery. Dotted every four feet or so along the lawn's edge, the rocks were an excellent skipping opportunity on my walk home from school—until the day I tripped on one and landed newly-minted-adult-front-teeth-first on the next. That might have been the sole occasion on which anyone in my family cursed the lack of neighbourhood sidewalks. Otherwise, the absence of a three-foot strip of concrete abutting every lot made that small section of the city seem more like an enchanted village, a tree-studded nook in the middle of an urban grid. Huge trees dominated the landscape; lots were divided by hedge-rows, not by fences. Every lawn wore a majestic arrangement of leaves and branches like a brooch: droopy willow boughs floated above garden rockery, thick spruce and statuesque firs guarded every front door on the block. Trees emblazoned property fronts as predictably as a driveway or a front stoop. I was four and a half years old the day I stood in the centre of that living room, leaned against the tree-trunk leg of a strict babysitter, and watched my parents' car emerge from the woodsy surroundings and pull into the driveway. My mother had been gone for a couple of days—I think that's why I paid such attention to her return. I can still conjure the distinct sense of unease I felt as I looked through the window. The interior of our house was warm, quiet, safe; outside it was cold, mid-November. I watched my father pull his coat closed against the chill as he stepped out of the car and stood beside the jack pine, pipe clenched between his teeth on the left side. (It was 1970; fathers smoked on their way home from the maternity ward.) Instead of coming straight up the stone walkway to the house, he crossed in front of the car to help my mother. Together, they lifted a small bundle from the back seat. I can still see it in slow motion. Football-sized cloth package, held gingerly and gazed at. What was that I read in their eyes—reverence? Awe? Joy? The profound delight that had once been reserved for me. The mutation of love into this divided state, rapid and invisible as cell division, fascinated me as I stared through the double-pane windows. I wasn't afraid, or even upset. But I was profoundly aware of the Change that had just pulled into the driveway—aware that life as I knew it was over. This was big—and irreversible. I was pretty sure I wanted whatever was coming, but the significance and permanence of this novelty item hit me like a medicine ball. My mother wore her wavy, raven hair just above shoulder length at the beginning of the 1970s, held back from her face with a stylish hairband, usually the same colour as her outfit. She liked to match. As I watched her belly swell under her A-line bold print dresses, I must have been regaled with that age-old positive spin campaign about the excitement that was to come, about the joys of having a little sibling to play with. Eventually I would indeed hold him and coo over him like a good big sister, and twenty-odd years later he would be the dude of honour at my wedding, my favourite person on earth. But in my final moments as an only child, alone in that tidy living room, I felt an overwhelming shift in my world view. In that moment, I grew older, more responsible, less carefree. When the front door opened, letting in a whisper of November's chill, I became a first-born. First-borns are beneficiary to the full force of life's longing for itself, as Kahlil Gibran called the yearning that brings a young couple into parenthood: the desire to repeat our best qualities and reinvent our weaknesses, to bestow new hope unto the world. We are the only ones in the birth order pattern to enjoy our parents' undivided devotion, for whatever length of time before the first sibling arrives. I had nearly five years' worth. My every move was documented, appraised, measured. A small off-white envelope holds the trimmings from my first haircut. Spiral-bound albums store a record of my first word, first friend, every birthday party guest list, prize ribbons no matter how small the race—even my first bus pass.

From the moment we first roll over to a chorus of cheering, first-borns learn that our actions yield results. Proud report cards; bulletin boards covered with medals, awards, certificates of accomplishment; leading roles in all the school plays. We could be forgiven for believing that our performance is equal to our worth. It's there in photographs of my own children: the wide-eyed insouciance of the rosy-cheeked baby, the sparkly impishness of the playful middle child, and the slightly more sober, duty-bound smile of the first-born—ever measured, even in a candid snapshot. I understand it the minute I look into my eldest son's eyes, gazing obediently toward the camera: the feeling that he has to get this moment right. In my own childhood photos, I am often standing at attention, clearly following the photographer's every directive. My summer-blond hair is straight, tidy; there exists only a handful of pictures in which it is not tied back with a colour coordinated bow. As an infant I sport lace-trimmed bonnets; as a toddler, buttercream-yellow smocked dresses, painstakingly hand-stitched by my mother; as a little girl, I was sent to photo-worthy occasions in dresses with matching handbags. Exactly what my mother thought a seven-year-old might need to carry in a navy floral-print handbag is not clear; form dominated function in my early sartorial situations. The primary objective was to appear proper, controlled, Just So.

———

THE HOUSEHOLD INTO WHICH I was born first had one defining characteristic: conservatism was more than a political stance. My father, a bespectacled lawyer who liked his cocktails served promptly and often argued that children were best seen and not heard, was unique among his cronies: he was mindful of conserving the earth's resources, as well as the bank's. My brother Jake and I were raised to turn the lights off when we left the room and to put on a sweater if we were cold. We knew to finish every drop of milk in the glass and to put our bicycles back in the garage so they wouldn't get rained on and rust. *"Rights come with responsibilities, young lady."* It was simply a sensible way to live; the planet never entered into the equation.

My ever-practical mother made conservation a household norm. Long before any logo was developed for the three *R* words, my family practised them religiously. We reduced: family friends used to joke that one didn't accept dinner invitations at the Deacons' after October unless one was prepared to bring a pair of slippers, since we didn't like to turn up the heat. We reused: paper mushroom bags from the grocery store went to school the next day carrying lunch. We recycled: labels were peeled off juice tins, both ends removed and the tins finally flattened under a sturdy shoe so mum could deposit them in the giant recycling domes in the A&P parking lot—why toss away something that still held value? I was raised on war baby logic: Waste Not, Want Not; my family conserved because it made sense.

By way of illustration, here is what it looked like when my mother met a chicken.

Purchased at the neighbourhood butcher, it was carried home, usually on foot. During this trip, an unspoken commitment was established, a pledge to take seriously this relationship between bird and cook.

After the chicken had been rinsed clean, a paste of freshly

mashed garlic was wedged beneath its fatty skin and half a lemon placed in its hollow centre. Lightly seasoned, the bird was then roasted to perfection. It was served with grace and warmth to the cook's hungry family, dumbfounded at their good fortune to be guests at such a sumptuous table.

When the meal was over and the bird had cooled, my mother's long, lean fingers poked with practised determination into each orifice, harvesting every crevice on the carcass, stripping the last strand of flesh from bone. The remaining bones, fat, cartilage, and sundry goo were collected in a stockpot and covered with water, peppercorns, parsley, carrot, leafy shafts of celery (stalks reserved), and unpeeled onions. The stock boiled then simmered under a careful watch; my mother's kitchen smelled like a fine French restaurant. Bones and mushy vegetable remains were strained, the liquid left to cool. Later, the crusty layer of hardened fat was skimmed from the top of the bowl. Cloudy, golden liquid was poured into old yogourt containers, which were labelled and stored in the freezer: chicken stock, which she would use as a base for soups and other recipes. Future hunger, meet present preparation.

But the cook was not done with that hen yet. Back to the remaining flesh, which was chopped into small squares for chicken salad. Mayonnaise, green onions, reserved celery stalks, a dash of Worcestershire. Tonight's dinner would yield tomorrow's lunch, maximizing value.

One bone was always held back from the stockpot: the wishbone, treasure of the carcass. The delicate V-shaped bone with a flattened knob at the centre was detached and hung on a cupboard knob to dry out overnight. The next day it was shared between the cook's two children, eager to see which end would pull in their favour; whoever snapped the side with the knob won the good luck.

That bird gave my mother everything it had, and she didn't waste an ounce.

Such patient, disciplined effort was a household norm; the state of Just So was not attained without hard work. Standards were held high both in and out of the kitchen.

"Look, Dad, I got 91 percent on my math test!" My green and gold uniform rumpled from after-school mischief, I burst breathlessly into the living room.

Snapshot: cream-coloured carpet, mantel sparingly adorned with heirloom silver candlesticks and matching antique plates, my father settled into the floral chintz armchair beside the fireplace. "What happened to the other nine points?" he'd say, peering over the newspaper with no more than a hint of a smile. "There's room for improvement, my dear. Room for improvement."

Rationally, I know that I had other conversations with my father in the nearly twenty years we cohabited, yet this is the one I recall with most sentiment attached, likely on account of the frequency with which it took place. Nearly every perceived success fell just short of praiseworthy. There is so much room for improvement in the world; no wonder I grew up feeling I had lots to do.

Four and a half years my junior, Jake was seldom my first choice of playmate, nor I his. But when circumstances left us no other options, we played together, usually with my brother's toys. Jake's toy collection evolved to match the shifts in 1970s popular culture. No staircase was safe passage for fear of slipping on a stray motorcycle during his obsession with Evel Knievel (once, when no amount of plunging would clear the clog in our toilet, a plumber was called. He found Evel Knievel, one of his "Spectacular Jumps" having lodged him deep in the closet bend of the drainpipe). Soon tri-colour motorcycles were replaced by landspeeders, Wookies, and Obi-Wan Kenobi. I dodged light sabre attacks on the way to my Holly Hobbie bedroom.

Most of his boy toys held minimal appeal for me, but I could always be lured into the imaginary play of building a miniature city with blocks. Jake had a sizable assortment building-shaped blocks: wooden squares and rectangles carved with windows and doors, with pointed rooftops painted red. Some of the houses were a pistachio green, some creamy yellow, others a dull white, in a variety of sizes, with a series of rectangular towers for architectural variety. Several of the large blocks had so many windows we took them to be hotels—or the rich people's houses. A few towers were painted with ornate windows, miniature church steeples.

When the weather trapped us inside, Jake and I would dump the bin of blocks onto the family room floor and build a city. We created Lilliputian streets, alleys, neighbourhoods, and parking lots. We populated our mini metropolis with ball-headed Fisher-Price people, painted with permanent smiles. To get them where they needed to go, we perched our small wooden humans on top of Hot Wheels roadsters, with steering wheels the size of their drivers' eyes—the mismatched scale mattered not.

On rare occasions, my mother would let us create a winter city, covering the entire floor of the room with white tissues. With uncharacteristic abandon, we were allowed to empty the entire Kleenex box. As I flattened each tissue into place, smoothing the snowy understorey for our miniature city, the transformation was pure magic. The brown and gold diamond pattern of the rough wool rug disappeared under a thin layer of white tissues, sanitizing the scene, creating a picturesque community that radiated purity and peace. I stood back and marvelled, relishing the tiny, perfect world we had created. Enjoying omniscience.

After a day or so, tissues would invariably shift out of place. Streets grew crooked, steeples toppled; our make-believe world lost its charm. Cleaning up the blocks was the easy part; houses, hotels, and skyscrapers alike were hastily tossed back into their bin. But the blanket of snow could not be thrown away with such easy abandon. Those tissues had to be folded, one by one, and put back into the Kleenex box—ninety-nine cents or not, we didn't waste.

———

MY FATHER DRESSED SHARPLY for his work at a downtown law firm: light wool suit, crisply pressed striped cotton shirt, coloured silk tie in a shade just bold enough to accent the thin strand of colour shot through the suit's grey check. The tie was usually subtly patterned with a tasteful hint of whimsy—the repeated motif of the shape of Martha's Vineyard, or a racing horse in mid-stride. I sometimes sat in his clothes cupboard and ran my fingers along the tie rack, a cascade of silk tresses, so many cheerful colours—hallmarks of the levity I so cherished in my otherwise strict disciplinarian father. His ties were a working man's cry of self-determination, offering up a clue to the imaginative, independent thinker belied by his otherwise standard-issue corporate uniform.

When I turned seventeen, my father realized that he could spare himself the ride home on a crowded subway and the long walk from the station: I became my father's chauffeur, an arrangement that suited both his increasingly arthritic knees and my newly licensed driver's enthusiasm for getting behind the wheel.

Travelling from his downtown office to our midtown home, I'd drive us north on one of the city's main arteries. Invariably, the flow of cars would thicken like a paste of metal and glass until we became mired altogether, gridlocked in rush hour. My father sat in the passenger seat, tie knot loosened, his cigar held out the window. On the stereo, the price I had to pay for being allowed to drive a car—jazz classics. Benny Goodman, Duke Ellington, Fats Waller; "The Joint Is Jumpin'," "Handful of Keys," "Don't Let It Bother You." *Listen to that piano playing, Gilly, just listen. Bloody marvellous.* Though the rhapsodic tinkling of ivories was a partial distraction from the stagnant pool of cars surrounding us, my father did not abide traffic jams. Most other homeward-bound commuters seemed content to sit in their discontent, idling in an automotive stew. Not my dad. Allergic to bottlenecks, he liked to outsmart congestion. *Turn right up here,* he'd say, *attagirl.* Onto this little east–west residential street? *Yes, my dear, we'll find a smarter way home. There must be a left along here somewhere, here we go. Look, this side street runs six blocks north. Turn right and we'll come out at the gas station, no wait, turn here so we avoid the stoplight. Hang a left onto the main street and we're home and dry. Attagirl, Gilly. We're way ahead of the crowd now. There's always another way to get where you're going.*

the secret path

THE FIRST TIME the earth's improvement popped onto my radar, I was a freshly minted university graduate and had recently made the humbling return to live with my parents. The first floor of our house was under renovation, so my resourceful mother had set up a makeshift kitchen in our basement, using the beer fridge, the laundry sink, and a microwave to get through culinary duties during several months of construction upstairs. While other families eat in restaurants or order takeout during months of renovation, my enterprising mother (cheered on by my cost-conscious father) prepared all home-cooked meals for weeks on end in our low-ceilinged basement—the dryer doubling as a chopping board, crackers and bananas nestling in beside the iron and fabric softener, the hot water heater droning as backdrop to any conversation. It was here in our cozy provisional scullery, eating breakfast on the patio furniture that constituted the temporary family meal table, that I first read a feature story in the newspaper about The Environmental Crisis. A physics professor from the University of Manitoba had written an article entitled "Is Man Meddling? If razing forests does cause drought, mankind must mend its ways, and soon." It went on to catalogue many of the climatic shifts that are now familiar fodder in global warming discussions. This was Al Gore redux: my first taste of uncomfortable, not to mention inconvenient, truths. I was flabbergasted. The more I read about the imperilled state of the planet, the more agitated I grew. Waste, mess, pollution, and lack of respect for nature's resources flew in the face of everything I had been raised to think of as normal. Something had to be done. I likely approached household chores such as recycling with more enthusiasm after that, hauling the new-fangled city-issued collection bins to the curb with a pleasing sense of virtue. And I dimly recall chastising my parents for the very occasional oversight of leaving the sprinkler on overnight, having appointed myself official monitor of all household water consumption.

What I do remember quite vividly as my first asser-tion of high-minded lifestyle choices was the next visit to my favourite pasta bar, not long after my environmental awakening. When asked what kind of sauce I'd like on my noodles, I replied, with instant conviction, "Vegetarian, please." I liked the sound the word made as it came out of my mouth, each consonant vibrating with certainty. And with that, I gave up eating meat and ticked it off a mental list of Steps in the Right Direction. I didn't know how to save the world in one fell swoop, but veggie spaghetti sauce seemed like a good place to start.

As every first apartment is, mine became a place to stretch and flex the muscles of my emerging identity. I took pains to incorporate every eco-friendly lifestyle choice I learned about: I brought empty jars to the health food store to buy ingredients in bulk, eschewed hot water at the laundromat, hung my laundry to dry. I rode my bicycle to work, where I pestered my colleagues to print on both sides of the page. The planet became a personal project; the more I learned, the harder I tried. Drawing on my mother's resourceful common sense and my father's allergy to waste, I reasoned that the human animal had better take some responsibility, starting with my own example. I imagine a thought bubble over my idealistic head as I continued to pore over dire planetary forecasts: "What can we do about this? How can we fix it?" I channelled Mickey Rooney's gee-whiz enthusiasm from the old musicals I knew so well as a theatre major: Come on kids, we can do it! With a little pluck and a lot of heart we can turn this ship around.

At the school where I worked as a tutor for children with learning disabilities, I taught them to celebrate Arbour Day. I pretended it was the Next Big Thing, an age-old day of nature-reverent ceremony that was coming back into vogue. Actually, I wasn't pretending. As I negotiated with nurseries to donate plant material, convinced a nearby seniors' residence to let us naturalize its landscape, twisted the arm of the school principal to let the students spend the afternoon getting their hands dirty planting shrubs and trees, I was on fire with conviction. This was just the beginning, I knew. As I surveyed the crowd of smiling children and teachers wiping dirt off each other, congratulating themselves on the lopsided shrubbery that now graced the previously barren lawn, I could feel change in the wind. My crusade had begun. Soon my career path steered me to a bigger platform, a public showcase of my quest for planetary improvement. As a radio broadcaster and later a television host at CBC News in Montreal, I interviewed artists, biologists, dancers,

researchers, conservationists, politicians, and engineers. The
conversation subjects ranged wildly over the years, but the
root points remained the same: tell us about how you are
fixing something that is broken or adding something missing
from our world; help make the audience care about the earth
we live on. While colleagues in the newsroom rode the escal-
ator up one flight to grab fuel from the cafeteria, I rode my
bicycle ten blocks to the market to buy fresh, whole ingredients and assembled a nutritious lunch at my desk. Before
organic gourmet hit the aisles of every grocery store, I was
the laughingstock of my workplace: alfalfa sprouts littering
my keyboard, a touch of avocado smeared on my notes.
Over time, I became the go-to gal for environmental awareness raising, making a living on camera and on podiums,
preaching the healthy eco-gospel. I wrote books cataloguing
all the changes consumers should make to their daily habits
to live a little lighter on Mother Earth. *Turn off the tap while
brushing your teeth to save water! Check your tire pressure
regularly to improve fuel efficiency! Set a timer in the shower
to reduce hot water consumption!* With doggone determination and tireless cheer, I penned articles and blogs about the
simple green ways I go about my life—most of it learned at
my mother's resourceful apron strings. I catalogued countless
instructions for order; an ounce of lateral thinking combined
with a pinch of extra effort was all it took. I told everyone who
would listen. It all seemed so *obvious*. There was a solution,
a remedy for our ailing environment: we just had to try a
little harder. The answers are all there, by gum, just read the
research! I incorporated the quest for Just So excellence with
the belief that I could really change the world if I tried hard
enough. I never really meant to become the poster girl for

sustainable living. It just happened. I ate nothing but plants, cleaned non-toxic, commuted on two wheels; I lived *right*. I trod the Secret Path.

That's what it felt like in my head: a route that mainstream folks weren't taking, or couldn't even see, that was a direct path to affordable health and happiness. The Secret Path was simply a series of clear and manageable choices that led me, and hopefully others who might follow my example, through the landmines of life: try a little harder, live a little lighter, and outsmart disaster. I trekked that side road for more than twenty years, chipper with self-satisfied conviction. Along the way, I met a fellow traveller. When Grant took his seat beside mine at my cousin's wedding, I heard rushing in my ears—the sound of love landing. Wavy brown hair, an electric smile, his sparkling brown eyes still glimmering with the thrill of some freshly taken risk; I knew he knew his way along the Secret Path. Grant was born third, the rebel of his family. His outside-the-box thinking drew me in immediately: this guy knew how wrong the world was and had the brilliance and passion to fix it. Plus he made me laugh.

Lying together on a creaky wooden dock at dusk one evening on a romantic lakeside tryst, we daydreamed about the future. About the environmental campaigns I would start, the school he'd run for kids from low-income families. We'd teach them music, art, and respect for the natural world. We'd build an army of the next generation who understood how to live lightly, to take care. We didn't dream of a big house with fancy cars in the driveway; we dreamed of making things right. This was my man.

Grant and I were married on the sun-warmed rock of my family's cottage island. I wore bare feet and a dress made by a clothing designer friend who is from the Dene First Nation; the dress bore appliquéd designs of the killer whale and the raven, symbols of loyalty and creativity, the themes of our union.

We had babies, one wide-eyed boy after another. Reggie, as a nod to family lineage, after my paternal grandfather Reginald; Harper, after Harper Lee, who created our favourite character in literature, Atticus Finch; and Miles, because it is an anagram for *smile*, his default repose since birth. Even our baby-naming rationale was prescriptive.

We swaddled them in natural fibres, eschewed plastic toys for untreated wood.

As our boys grew I tickled their toes with the "This little pig" rhyme, only the little pig on the penultimate toe ate tofu, instead of roast beef. (Ridiculous, I know, but I will say that those grown boys now eat the pressed soybean product without hesitation, as well as any other vegetable you can throw at them.) When I began to introduce solid food to my breastfed babies, I recoiled at the thought of contaminating their innocent selves with any impurities, so I steamed and puréed organic vegetables by the basketful. (I recall more than one occasion on which my father howled obscenities as he searched our freezer in vain for ice to cool his Jack Daniels; every ice cube tray was filled with puréed squash.) When my first-born, Reggie, started kindergarten, I bundled the younger two into some multi-wheeled stroller contraption and pushed them up and down the hilly walk to the neighbourhood school, every day. Local school? Check. Fresh air and exercise? Check. There were a number of rainy-day occasions when I cursed my conviction, and a number of snowsuit-induced tantrums wherein they cursed it themselves. But I wouldn't dare contribute to the climate change crisis just to get my kids to school in the morning. So I dug in and made us all walk; my virtuousness compensated for my discomfort.

What is the modern woman's interpretation of perfect? Defined by body image or dental track record, I'm out; my bulgy belly and capped front tooth are hideous disqualifiers. Defined by punctuality, I'm also a dark horse, unable as I am to get to where I'm going any less than ten minutes late, no matter how hard I try. Defined by tidiness and meticulous grooming—people who know me are laughing too hard right now to read any further.

The kind of perfection some of us, especially mothers, are after is characterized by a list of informed choices, executed with dedication and perseverance: Child-friendly, fresh, homemade, chemical-free, organic, plastic-free, natural, locally sourced. Careful. Mindful. Respectful. Safe. All signposts along the Secret Path. In the muddle of work–life balance, if we are on top of things, establish mastery over one small corner of the bedlam, and do everything right, we can ensure the best outcome.

Here is what it looks like: Smeared across my armpits each morning is a homemade natural deodorant—lemon oil and cornstarch paste; no petrochemicals seeping into my pores. Strangers in the grocery store parking lot stare at me as I load my bicycle baskets with produce and hard goods, then careen home like a circus clown, an improbable feat of balance; no fossil fuels emitted from my errand runs. Underneath my kitchen sink, a parade of edible cleansers: tea tree oil, baking soda, distilled vinegar, lavender spray. Second-hand clothing is all my children know—thank god

I had boys. My bank balance teeters at the red zone, not from new electronics or exotic travel, but organic, local food. Our family of five went carless for four months waiting for a hybrid car that we could afford (and fit into) to come onto the market. I menstruate into a reusable silicone cup, hand out fair-trade organic chocolate on Halloween, and sleep on unbleached organic cotton bedsheets. I do not live in a hemp tent and forage for berries; I am an urban environmentalist, doing what I can.

You needn't call yourself an environmentalist to see how the planet shifts before our very eyes—we can only imagine what consequences our children will suffer as they reach adulthood in a less hospitable climate. In the meantime, they tumble in the back door rosy-cheeked after a day of play, their downtown lungs just a little more benzene-soaked than the day before. Another species disappears, rainforests shrink, water sources become contaminated. Industry pollutes, governments dither, consumption rages on; the dread of a ravaged planet can drown you in an instant. Good thing I found the Secret Path. I cannot be choked alive in a polluted, industrial greed-fest (or as the Lorax would say, Thneed-fest) so long as I continue my personal crusade. If I work hard enough at it, I keep the fear at bay. Every planet-saving trick sparked a flint of hope in the darkness of global ills; the cocktail of non-toxic cleaning, healthy eating, and outdoorsy living became medicinal, an inoculation against doom. "Every revolution begins with the slightest shift!" I preached from the stage to crowds of potential green converts. "Imagine the ripple effect your actions will have in your communities as you slowly begin to shift your consumer patterns. When the marketplace changes, business and governments respond. And when that happens, ladies and gentlemen, we have changed the world." The sheer enthusiasm for a footprint-shrinking life-style became a source of hope and faith for me. I believed my own message—how could I not? It tingled all the way down to my toes. Start to change the way you shop, the way you pack your children's school lunches, the way you get from A to B, and watch the way you shift the culture. Saving the earth will save you money and make you healthier—it's an infectious promise. I renewed my pledge every day. Those who subscribe to healthful strategies feel emboldened by our resourcefulness, smugly convinced we know better and will be rewarded for our efforts. We believe passionately that there is a right way to live, to mitigate against disaster on every scale; we cling to that hope as to a willow bough suspended over fierce whitewater. Do we believe we can outrun fate?

littered with despair

THE BEE POPULATION dropped by 26 percent last year. Honeybees pollinate a third of all the food we eat and contribute an estimated fifteen billion dollars in annual agriculture revenue to the U.S. economy.

Albert Einstein once said, "If the bee disappears from the surface of the earth, man would have no more than four years to live. No more bees, no more pollination, no more plants, no more animals ... no more man."

And that's just the bees. The eight warmest years on earth since 1880 have all occurred since 2001; the concentration of carbon dioxide in the atmosphere has nearly doubled since 1900. Floods, tsunamis, and droughts dominate the headlines, growing in frequency and intensity. Trees, thirsty for carbon dioxide, are logged 'round the clock, both illegally and with clearcut abandon, to meet our insatiable demand for growth. With fewer trees to clear the air, smog-related deaths outnumber cancer-related deaths—the World Health Organization estimates that two million people die prematurely each year from exposure to air pollution. In 1908, the Ford Model T got twenty-five miles to the gallon; today, the average car gets sixteen. Idling your car for more than ten seconds uses more gas than turning it off and restarting when you're ready to drive away, yet everywhere I look drivers sit in idle, polluting the air, wasting gas. Sometimes I muster the nerve to ask them to stop. Heart pounding faster as I approach the car, I summon leadership, courage. *This is for my children.* Still I tremble, wondering how the stranger at the wheel may react to my suggestion. I catch their eye, flick my wrist back and forth, hoping that is universal code for "Please turn off your ignition." Occasionally a smile, a nod, a turning off; more often a middle finger, a tuning out. *Diabetes rates have risen sharply if you track the rise in pesticide use since the end of the Second World War and track the rise in cancer rates you'll notice an eerie parallel farmed fish are fed genetically modified meal and swim in their own feces toxic heavy metals bioaccumulate in the body and in the food chain urban sprawl creates car-dependent communities manufacturers operate with built-in obsolescence policies when viewed from space the highest point of land on the Eastern seaboard of North America is a landfill site*—anger, exasperation, anxiety, and outrage are occupational hazards for the environmentalist. This emotionally fraught landscape, littered with doom and despair, is where I live. Stuck in traffic on a busy highway at midday I am dumbfounded anew at the number of combustion engines on the road, at the number of roads, at the soulless suburban factories employing all the drivers. Sunlight illuminates the haze of smog; I cannot see a single tree in any direction. The gloom of a gluttonous world threatens to depressurize the air and crush in the car windows. My lungs cannot hold the outrage.

twisted roots across the path

MILES IS IN MY BELLY, doing cartwheels. I lie back on my bed and gaze down as ripples of motion undulate across my burgeoning paunch. My brother always got a kick out of seeing those movements during my first two pregnancies. Our long-standing basement tenant, he was often the first person around to witness a significant phase during my first years as a parent. In fact, Jake is more intimately connected with pregnancies and early childhood stages than I suspect most single uncles are. His apartment door is seldom closed; drooling toddlers welcome. If ever Reggie or his little brother, Harper, grows weary of rolling Hot Wheels down the ironing board or hearing Raffi on loop, they patter to the basement stairs, cast me a pleading glance, then promptly turn their bulbous cloth-diapered bottoms around to back down the stairs on all fours. The bachelor's cave is filled with endless fascination for small boys: beer bottle collection, reclining swivel chair, large dog, and best of all, big uncle Jakie. "Hi, Boss!" he beams, then wrestles each boy into a warm embrace in his strong, rugby-player's arms. Other occasions, when only the hearing-impaired could have missed the thunderous approach of those stocky little legs thundering down the stairs, Jake feigns delighted surprise at their attempts to scare him with a "Boo!" No babysitter was ever more beloved, and, it must be said, none more taken advantage of. But for weeks now Jake's apartment has been empty. I check the clock. 7:05—time to pick up the phone. The evening shift nurses will have just come on duty at the hospital in Vancouver where my brother lies in a semi-comatose state. I've had better luck with the evening nurses; they don't put me on hold for as long. They know who Jake Deacon is as soon as I call. I hear the clack of their heels marching down the corridor ... pause ... the shuffle to sidestep a squeaky food trolley ... then the clack resumes. Some nights I try to count the footsteps to gauge the length of the corridor. My brother's room is at the farthest remove from the seventh floor nursing station, in the Infectious Disease ward of the Vancouver General Hospital. A weekend trip to Vancouver over a month ago went awry: a pattern of symptoms that began on the airplane led him first to a walk-in clinic, then to emergency. As the misdiagnoses mounted, he eventually became an inpatient. MRI. Blood work. Spinal tap. Ultrasound 1. Ultrasound 2. More blood work, another spinal tap. A parade of Infectious Disease residents passes through weekly, studying the mystery that is my thinning, ever-weakening brother. A firm diagnosis eludes them all. Meningitis? Prostatitis? West Nile virus? The impulse to remedy is my first response. I was born first; shouldn't I shoulder some responsibility for getting him through this? But I am powerless to help, prevented by my pregnancy from entering an Infectious Disease ward. So every night I call, hoping to thrust wellness at him through the telephone. The narrowest of connections, it is my only means of input into his fog; I desperately squash succour and strength into a tiny parcel and shove it along those sound waves. I imagine sparks of colour and ripples of song tripping across the landscape along old-fashioned telephone lines. The sole person who understands exactly where I came from and what I'm made of is sick, possibly dying, but my own blessings of future happiness prevent me from doing anything about it. Helplessness is an unfamiliar feeling for me, as foreign a concept as failure; I lie on my bed two thousand miles away and will him to get better. The clacking stops, a muffled voice speaks gently, querying wakefulness. Perhaps his back is to her, rolled onto his side, curly hair flattened, half asleep. His glazed eyes stare into middle space. This I can hear in his voice when he takes the phone, several long-distance minutes since the call was first answered. "Hey, bro. How are you today?" A pause. "Hey." Another. "I'm okay, I guess." He knows who I am, but little enthusiasm registers in his voice. Groggy and weak, he answers my questions with minimal output. There is nothing to say. He is not feeling better. The same as he felt yesterday. Neck hurts. Tired. Not hungry. Prognosis remains unclear. Only he doesn't articulate all that detail. He just grunts monosyllabic replies to my questions, the same ones as yesterday. I hang up and resume my soak in a stew of agitation, desperate to fix his brokenness. But I cannot. The box of tissues beside my bed is gone, used up after last night's call. Tears and snot crest my upper lip, run into my mouth. Tears of fear taste saltier than tears of sorrow; control, fear's righteous stepchild, makes me choke, exasperated.

———

SIX WEEKS INTO this cruel and unlabelled dismantling of his spirits, my brother had regained just enough strength to let my mother put him on an airplane and bring him home to our basement apartment. He had lost forty pounds, a little bit of his memory, and most of his strength. So when he returned to health several months later, it was with renewed vigour and determination to catch up on the life he had missed. Marching steadfastly away from the suffering that had so frightened those who love him most, Jake got a girl-friend, got an MBA, got engaged, got a house, got married, got pregnant. Accomplishments and life milestones fell into place like a series of meticulously lined-up dominoes. Just So. But the pregnancy didn't last. Nor would the next, nor the one after that. My brother had outrun weakness, but not heartache.

There was a summer when my brother's wife, Sara, was pregnant. Joyful anticipation buoyed the family's collective spirits with every passing week her belly swelled. My boys fought over who would play net when they taught their baby cousin to play hockey; my mother pulled pale blue blankets out of storage to be washed, ones she had saved since my brother was wrapped in their flannel warmth; my sister-in-law wept at commercials for fabric softener, a sure sign her hormones were working overtime, building new life. Weeks passed in this rousing state—nineteen to be exact. One morning in August, while on vacation at the family cottage on a small island in the Ottawa River, I headed down the path through the woods to cross to the mainland for a morning jog. At the crest of the island, a cedar tree grows crookedly amidst scrubby brush. Just behind it, stepping onto the uneven rock, I saw Jake. His wife was right behind him.

"Hey! What a surprise! What are you guys doing here?"

Jake is a master of the unforeseen; he takes tremendous pleasure in staging unanticipated visits and gifts—he must be up to his old tricks, I reckoned, joining us for a surprise summer weekend on the river. I hurried toward them with my arms in the air, but stopped suddenly. My delight at their unannounced visit vanished as I saw the anguish in Jake's eyes; the tears streaming down Sara's crumpled face. "No!" I moaned quietly at first, hoping I had misapprehended their wretchedness. Jake's lower lip flattened into a grimace of suffering. "We got some test results," he managed. "Bad news." The inside of his throat crumpled like a dry paper bag, his voice ran out of air. "No! No! Noooooooo ..." My cry was feral; sound issued directly from my gut, bypassing the controlled precision of vocal chords.

We took each other in our arms, a collection of heaving shoulders. Jake sobbed out further details. Neural tube defects. Unbelievably rare. Forced termination. I broke away from their arms and kicked the rock as hard as I could. "Fuck you!" I screamed skyward. "Fuck you, fuck you, fuck you! Why?" I pounded the nearby cedar with a closed fist. After a few minutes of wailing in despair, I was drained; my raging protestations dried up, leaving just the sour pulp of misery. Jake and I helped Sara to the ground; her full belly was still cumbersome, in spite of being untenable. We sat together on the hard, lumpy rock, weeping quietly. I picked at the moss lining the rock under my legs, ripping it into smaller and smaller pieces until it was small enough to grind into a powder between my first finger and thumb. Fix this; make the problem go away. Make it Just So, dammit. Reflexively, my mind scrambled for a solution, something no one had thought of. I howled inside, desperate to solve the problem. The disharmony of my brother's fertility challenge roared, cacophonous, in my ears. Running alone through wooded trails later that morning, I flew on the energy of outrage. Why had I been so lucky, so easily impregnated, so blessed with healthy children? Had I won the wishbone pull more often? I struggled to recall if our family chicken ritual had heralded the beginnings of this sibling imbalance.

My legs pumped at a record pace, running away from my guilt. Why could my brother not share in such good fortune? Tall trees whipped past in my peripheral vision. White pine, Jack pine, silver birch, spruce. Why did fate continue to trip Jake up? My legs pounded into the dry dirt layered with brown pine needles, skipped over twisted roots that lay across the path. I ran further into the woods, as fast as I could go. The route widened and brightened into a clearing; I slowed to a stop and bent over, panting. Breakfast lurched in my stomach, threatening to reappear. The morning sun beat down on my back and warmed the cool sweat pooling under my nylon shirt. I moved further down the trail, out of the clearing, back into the shade.

Of course I was healthy and happy, I reasoned; the first-born child shoulders blessings like confetti. All the health, happiness, and providence in my life took on a sour aspect, like the bile swirling around my morning meal, my stomach still heaving with the effort of the run. Joy that cannot be shared is colourless, devoid of fanfare. My heart felt blackened with the sorrow of injustice. I tilted my head skyward and screamed a dark, guttural cry through the roof of branches, "Why Jake? Why, for fuck's sake, does all the bad stuff have to happen to Jake?"

I wanted so goddamn badly to wrestle the joystick of power out of whoever's ignorant hands were steering fate at that moment; how I burned just to reach beyond the clouds and rewrite the lines of the script, before the ink dried on my brother's bad news.

Silently, naively, I begged for balance. It never occurred to me I might be inviting my own misfortune.

inconceivable

WHEN I FIRST FOUND a lump in my left breast I didn't really think much of it. I was with Grant in Peru on a working holiday, travelling down the Amazon on a riverboat and writing about the experience for a travel magazine. The editor of the magazine envisioned a piece about an enviro-activist's journey to Eco Ground Zero, a place where I could visit the mother of all environmental concerns. It was there, on a boat floating down the world's largest river through the most ecologically sensitive region on earth, that I discovered the lump that would make me question my earth-saving antics altogether.

When we got home from the Amazon, I used the excuse of my busy life with a freelance career and three children—ages ten, eight, and five—as the reason to ignore the lump. I had a planet to save: speeches to deliver, school fundraising projects to organize and lead, cold-water-washed laundry to sort, writing deadlines to meet, hungry boys to nourish with homemade healthy meals, abs to crunch into shape, countertops to wipe with vinegar ... my world-beating productivity allowed not a moment to contemplate weakness. Besides, in 2002 I had found a lump in the same breast that turned out to be a cyst, a fluid-filled sac not uncommon in many women's breasts. Cysts come and go with hormonal cycles and don't cause any pain. I convinced myself that's all this was, just another gristly, sinewy anomaly in my lumpy, cyst-prone breasts. No big deal.

But my husband (third-born of six) runs at a slower pace. He convinced me to get it checked out. So on a Monday morning I called my doctor's office to say I had found a lump in my breast. They saw me in a matter of hours. Our youngest son Miles was home, so he came along to the appointment.

My regular doctor was away; her replacement was a soft-spoken brunette with delicate fingers and a gentle touch. Checking my patient history, she noted the 2002 ultrasound that showed cysts, but she thought this lump felt different, a little too hard to be a cyst. I tried to interpret her facial expressions, her tone, her degree of concern, but I didn't know her well enough. I was fairly sure I sensed worry in her eyes, something approaching sadness for this young, otherwise healthy mother with a sweet young child, about to learn very bad news. A clamp of fear clutched my throat as we rode the elevator down from her office; I stared into that blank middle space as tears rolled silently down my hot cheeks on the subway ride home. I have cancer, I thought. I am going to die. This beautiful child, whose little hand held mine as we swayed along with the rattling subway train, will grow up without his mother. His brilliant, handsome, sensitive father will find another wonderful woman to share his life, and she will raise my children.

Somehow this didn't feel like my melodramatic tendency talking. Truth lands in the gut like a stone.

My favourite photograph of Miles: he is standing in my mother's kitchen after a family Christmas dinner, not quite two. He wears light blue fuzzy pyjamas, the kind with feet and a full-length zipper. His tufts of strawberry-blond hair have no weight; they buzz directly upward and outward from his skull, as though he has just touched a Van de Graaff generator. His cheeks are rosy red, flushed from a late night in a warm kitchen; his eyes, bright circles that match his blue suit, are looking right at the camera, as though pleased to find it there. He is colourful as candy. The picture is slightly out of focus: an impressionist's rendering of sweetness. That photo always stops me as I leaf through family albums; the joyous light that is my small fuzzy boy.

———

STEPPING ONTO THE STREETCAR for the last leg of our trip home, Miles and I were smacked in the face with the stench of toxic chemicals. The woman sitting in the front seat of the streetcar had just painted her fingernails; she waved her outstretched hands back and forth in front of her, fanning the fresh polish until it set.

"No wonder I have cancer," I mumbled to myself. "Our world is full of chemicals."

At that time I was neck-deep in research about hazardous ingredients in personal care products for an upcoming book—what would become *There's Lead in Your Lipstick: Toxins in Our Everyday Body Care and How to Avoid Them.* Working at my desk, my head spun on a daily basis with the shocking evidence about health concerns linked to toxic ingredients and about how no one tests them for human safety before they are introduced into the marketplace.

"It doesn't matter that I take care of myself and eat well," I thought. "There are toxins making their way into my bloodstream every minute. Things I never gave permission to enter my body are being put there every day by our industrial society. No wonder I'm about to die ..."

"Mama!" I turned to see Miles wincing. "You're hurting me!" I loosened my ratchet-tight grip of anxiety from around his small hand.

———

MY HUSBAND TRIED to reassure me that my imagination was spinning wildly, but I couldn't banish the fear of what the next week's tests might reveal. I called my doctor friend Gina. "Let me contextualize this situation for you," she reasoned. "You are a forty-two-year-old woman with no history of breast cancer on your mother's side. You breastfed three children, have not eaten meat in over twenty years, you are a runner, a yogi, and a cyclist who has a history of cystic breasts. I think it's wise that your doctor booked a mammogram and ultrasound. They may even do a biopsy to double-check the situation, but you really need to keep your fear in perspective."

A plausible narrative, one I could hold on to. So I bought in. With the mastery of an illusionist, I suppressed the grim narrative taking shape in my mind. As quickly as death's sudden foreboding had pierced the sheath of my stalwart disposition, I wrapped that unease in a red silk handkerchief and made it disappear. It was just another cyst, of course it was. I had to believe all was well and would remain thus. The script where I was in control was the only one I had rehearsed; any other plot line was inconceivable.

———

NUTS, EGGS. What else? *Green apples, tofu ...*

At some point during the course of a busy day (is there any other kind?) I typically conduct a mental audit of the refrigerator's contents, which in turn means tabulating a mental shopping list for what is missing. Mental shopping lists, though, absent any paper on which to write them down, are fleeting, shape-shifting things for a woman over forty; crystal clear one moment, evaporated like so much fog the minute we cross the grocer's threshold. A sensible person—say, my mother—would commit the list to print. Yet somehow writing it all down feels too easy; I prefer the age-defying cerebral gymnastics of memorization. My standard trick for total errand recall is to spell a word with the first letter of each item on the list—and then hope that I can remember what each letter stands for. Occasionally I bring home tomatoes instead of thyme, but for the most part the system is quite reliable.

One particular day while awaiting biopsy results, my shopping list was quite short. Nuts, eggs, green apples, tofu. I began to arrange the letters into a word ... *N.E.G.A.T.—holy shit.* My shopping list acronym spelled out more than half of the word "negative." Was it a sign? It must be a sign! If only I could figure out what else we might need that started with *I, V,* and *E,* I felt certain I could channel a message from the universe about my test results. *See!* I told myself, *you'll be fine—*my shopping list acronym was proof. Obviously fate was sending me a message through my groceries.

This wasn't the only time before or since that I have chosen to interpret coincidences in my day as messages from a parallel universe. All but the most cynical among us feel the enticing pulls of kismet once in a while. Perhaps they make us feel less alone, less like our good deeds can go entirely unrewarded, less adrift in the arbitrariness of fortune. They seem to offer up clues to having chosen the correct route through a given day, anchors to the comfort of being looked out for.

We had a freezer full of ice cream, and I couldn't think of anything else starting with *I*. With more than a little desperation, I combed through the kitchen in my mind's eye. We were, in fact, running low on celery, so I added it to the list since the shape of the stalk resembles the letter *I*. (Feeble, but honest—one must be legit when steering the force of the universe.) But I couldn't think of any gaps in the pantry that started with *V*. And in the end, the hands of fate could not be stopped by mnemonics. If only we had needed vinegar and eggplant.

optics of order

FOR A FRIDAY NIGHT dinner party at seven o'clock, my mother has the table set by Thursday at two-thirty. Arranged neatly upon the gleaming polished oak are the horse-themed placemats, the freshly ironed cream-coloured linen napkins (my mother says "serviettes" are made of paper and meant for picnics), the heirloom silver (salad fork on the outside), and the lead crystal wine-glasses. (There's lead in your lipstick *and* in your crystal.) Her signature touch, for every festive occasion she hosts, is to create a floral centrepiece of the kind seen in Renaissance paintings: an exquisite arrangement, each flower placed in precise position to achieve maximum visual splendour. My mother took classes through her garden club to master the craft, but she has natural talent and a way with flowers that no amount of hobby coursework could teach. She is gentle, patient, attuned to the shape and pulse of every living bloom. Flowers are her art form, brush and canvas both. If this ornate scene smacks of wealth, let me adjust the set: my mother also collects peanut butter packets and tea bags from airplanes, squirrelling them away in her purse along with thrice-used tissues and a miniature measuring tape for unplanned measurement-taking. When she comes to visit our house, she sometimes brings a bread bag filled with rotten fruit and vegetable scraps, as her condominium building does not participate in the municipal composting service. Once and always, a war baby: incapable of waste, attentive to any opportunity to shore up the stockade, taking prudent, sensible steps to prepare in the event of potential crisis.

Julia Child taught my mother how to cook a chicken, but it was Martha Stewart who earned the title of ultimate domestic inspiration, with her trifecta of talents: food, decor, and planning. My mother has always been quite a devotee of Martha Stewart and her cohort of style mavens—a kinship born of a shared fondness for planning. My mother surrounds herself with magazines, guidebooks, and television programs detailing how to establish order and beauty in every household setting. Gwyneth Paltrow, Debbie Travis, and other Martha descendants have built empires out of doing what my mother does for free: attending to domestic detail with a zeal for order, preparedness, and beauty, staving off the confusion and bewilderment of disharmony. All of them, on very different scales, strive for the optics of perfection. To each, it matters what other people think.

While I have managed to kill nearly every bit of plant material ever to cross the threshold into my home and have never been clear on the proper positioning of the salad fork, I am nonetheless my mother's daughter. How many of us reject our mother's aesthetic, only to replicate her deeper programming? My style may be different but I am programmed with the same imperative: the optics of order remain critical.

live lightly, take care

"UNPLUG THE DISHWASHER!" Harper hollered earnestly. "Uh, sweetie, we can't really do that. The plug is buried somewhere underneath the countertop." His six-year-old face fell; his eyes, the colour of perfectly-cooked toast, studied me with suspicion. "But we won't turn it on, okay?" I assured him. "It won't be using any energy if it's not turned on." Satisfied, he resumed his keener's tour of the house, flicking off every possible electrical device, preparing our home for Earth Hour. In 2007, a freakishly high percentage of the citizens of Sydney, Australia, powered down in unison as a sixty-minute gesture of solidarity toward battling climate change. It was a simple salute to the planet, catchy and easy to get behind. The rest of the world fell in love with the media-friendly campaign, and by 2008 there were fifty million people flicking off lights across thirty-five countries. One hour of energy reduction hardly adds up to much in light of our gargantuan and ever-growing consumption the other 8,764 hours of the year. But it's a place to start, and for those of us trying to give the earth a voice it is a brief window of gratification, when households the world over seem to share our values. One year before I would discover that suspicious knot in my breast tissue, World Wildlife Fund, the global conservation organization, decided to embrace the Earth Hour event in a big way; as a long-standing member of their board of directors, I joined in with the stunt. I talked it up at the dinner table in the preceding days. My children learned about it in school, discussing conservation strategies and what household appliances to power off during the event. In addition to the pedagogical potential, this was a great opportunity to show our kids that mum and dad weren't the only eco-nuts in the tree. At nine, six, and four, my boys were still young enough not to question the atypically green household they were growing up in. They didn't know that other people thought we were weird for making homemade yogourt. They knew why we hung our clothes to dry (to save energy!) and why mama was a vegetarian (meat production causes greenhouse gas emissions!) and why we didn't put plastic in the dishwasher (toxic phthalates are released when exposed to heat!). We walked to school, rain or shine, because driving was a waste of energy and caused air pollution. We ate organic, composted, printed on both sides of the page, had low-flow showerheads, shopped at the local farmers' market, washed our windows with club soda (okay, we didn't actually wash our windows all that often ...). Too young to rebel, my boys had drunk the Kool-Aid; they were on board for all these planet-saving shenanigans. So the chance to take part in an action campaign that reinforced our values was a point of pride. Just weeks before this particular Earth Hour, my first book had been released. *Green for Life* was an exhaustive guide to everyday lifestyle changes, full of tips and tricks for living lighter on the earth. It offered the same kind of upbeat, simple greening advice that filled my monthly column in a national women's magazine: use a low-flow showerhead to save water; wash laundry in cold water and hang to dry—and don't forget to empty the lint trap! Send your kids to school with reusable, litterless lunch containers! By this point you could find *Going Green with Gill Deacon* videos on television and all over YouTube, in which I mixed homemade vegetable wash to remove pesticide residue, tested appliances for energy efficiency, or demonstrated how to avoid water waste in a toilet. I had a reputation to uphold, this and every hour. Turning off the lights? Easy. We would see that challenge and raise it. Which was why, at a quarter to the appointed hour of darkness, Harper was hungrily scouring the house for more things to power down.

Meanwhile, Grant wasn't buying it. "This whole event is bullshit," he announced emphatically. "This planet is in serious peril and here we are getting all hyped up about a measly hour of contrived nonsense. People need to make serious behaviour change for true conservation, not waste time and creativity on an artificial gesture that goes nowhere." He can be a bit of a downer on occasion. Smart, passionate, and often right as rain, but a downer, nonetheless. Muttering his disapproval as the stroke of eight-thirty approached, Grant retreated to the top floor of our house, where he could wallow in his cynicism and indignation. From there he had a view of the city skyline, so he could watch to see how many office towers went dark, testing his theory that this was a pathetic consumer affectation with no real roots of meaningful change. Undeterred by his skepticism, I gathered my boys together and planned a cozy evening of pioneer living. I ran a shallow bath and the boys piled in. At eight-thirty on the nose, we flicked off the last of the lights and lit the candles. To carry the candles safely from room to room, we had dug out a few of our summer patio lanterns. We really had thought of everything. The bathroom glowed, a magical den. Huddled together in this small, warm room, we talked about what it might have been like to live in "the old in days" before electricity. Swaddling them in towels, their rosy cheeks damp and radiant, I felt connected to my maternal forebears; this was primal motherhood, stripped of modern distractions. My heart swelled to think that this enchanted evening, the mood set by flickering flame, would be shaping their souls, creating memories, and laying down our values: live lightly, take care. By about nine o'clock, my dewy lads were ready for bedtime stories. Carrying the lanterns down the hall from the bathroom, we realized that their cheap design was meant for sitting in one place; their flimsy wire handles became too hot to hold once the candles were lit. I found a couple of cloth napkins (no tree-killing paper napkins for us!) to wrap around the handles, and we made our way to the master bedroom. Setting the lanterns down on each of the bedside tables, we all piled into the queen-sized bed for story time. In spite of the eye strain from trying to read in such dim light, I was overcome by the idyll of the evening: sharing simple pleasures together and believing we could make a difference for the earth. My righteous eco-heart skipped a beat. I wasn't more than a page or so into the reading before Harper began to shift uncomfortably to my right. "Ah, mum?" "Yes, darling, what is it?" I asked in the gentlest whisper, my eyes still squinting at the page. "Ah, mum, your clock radio is on fire." Turning suddenly to look past my snuggled offspring, I saw that the upright handle of the lantern on the bedside table had collapsed to one side, depositing the cloth napkin directly into the flame. From there, the blaze had spread to my white plastic clock radio, which was now, indeed, ablaze. I leapt from my bed, inadvertently elbowing one child in the head and squashing the legs of another. "Ow!" they shrieked, as much hurt as they were frightened, with a good measure of disappointment thrown in, the reverie of our charmed evening shattered by the smouldering of melting plastic. Yanking the clock radio's cord from the wall socket, I set about trying to pick it—and the now flaming lantern—up without setting myself on fire. The snooze button sizzled, percolating bubbles of blistering plastic; noxious smoke puffed from the radio, a plume of hazardous gases billowing into my face as I rushed toward the bathroom. Holding my breath, I plunged the whole flaming lot into the bathtub. I heard my husband thundering down the stairs. Alerted by the children's shrieks, he had descended in a flash. "Jesus Christ, what happened? It smells like a chemical fire!" He began to flick on every light in the house as he rushed to air out the bedroom, fumbling with deadbolts to open porch doors, hurtling open windows with the abandon of June on this frigid March evening. "But it's only 9:06!" I kept thinking. There would be people outside in the park across the street from our house right now, out for a stroll, surveying the darkness of the neighbourhood, making mental notes of who was supporting the earth this hour. And who wasn't. "Open the back windows, get a cross-draft going!" Grant was yelling. "Kids, breathe into your sleeves! Those are toxic fumes coming off the melting plastic radio!" *"Doesn't Gill Deacon live there?"* they would be thinking. Losing faith in my commitment, losing hope for the cause, losing trust in my ability to save the earth. My lights were on, my windows were wide open, my furnace was working double time to keep the house warm, and my children were breathing in toxic fumes. Scanning the dark streets nervously as I wished away the remaining moments until nine-thirty, I prayed that no one was watching.

coincidence

THE SHARP JAB of a punch biopsy probe the size and shape of a knitting needle into the softly curved underside of my breast marked the turning point between calling that cell mass a lump and calling it a tumour. That may be the single moment that signalled the abrupt tack from living a life to fearing for its loss.

The doctor had scheduled a mammogram and ultrasound, standard issue follow-up for a lump like the one I was carrying around, just as Gina had assured me. Based on her professional encouragement, so convinced was I that a forty-two-year-old vegetarian earth mother couldn't possibly have anything more than a cyst lurking in her bosom, I chose, instead of fear, to approach the tests with the pragmatic pluck of the overachieving first-born. A deadline for the *There's Lead in Your Lipstick* manuscript loomed over my head, so I wanted to make the best use of my time, even at a medical appointment. What I anticipated would be long drawn-out periods in the hospital waiting room would be prime opportunities to get through the research book I was reading. As it turned out, no sooner had the kindly purple-vested volunteer greeted me and made what must have been her standard panini press joke, than I was whisked off for my mammogram. From there, I was taken directly to the ultrasound room down the hall, a dimly lit space with a high padded table and a lot of tubes of blue gel. It only occurred to me later that I should have been concerned about the haste with which I was being delivered from test to test; at the time, I was more anxious about getting to do some hospital-standard waiting so I could pull out my research. Finally, as I lay on the ultrasound table having undergone the initial massage with the cold blue gel, the technician told me I'd have to wait a few minutes while she located the doctor. "Would you like a magazine?" she offered. "Thank you, but no, I brought something to read," I replied brightly, and asked her to pass me my purse, from which I pulled out my copy of *Not Just a Pretty Face: The Ugly Side of the Beauty Industry*.

Stacy Malkan's chronicle of the birth of environmental health investigations into cosmetics ingredients is the *sine qua non* for every conversation about toxic chemicals in beauty products. I pulled the skimpy blue gown up over my shoulder, a vain attempt at warmth, and tried to ignore the chill on my gel-coated breast. Propping myself up with my purse, an unsympathetic pillow, I opened the book to the page where I had left off at my last reading: *Chapter 6, Pinkwashing*. The chapter went on to explain the pink-washing practices of several companies that invest heavily in breast cancer awareness marketing campaigns and other pink ribbon promotions while manufacturing products that contain chemicals with known links to breast cancer. But it was the first sentence of that chapter that struck me like a speeding downtown bus: "In the last twenty years, more American women have died from breast cancer than the number of Americans killed in the First World War, the Second World War, the Vietnam War and the Korean war combined." Maybe I should have just read a magazine.

It wasn't long before the doctor arrived, smeared my goose-pimpled breast with more cooling gel, and examined the lump through the eyes of her ultrasound wand. Within minutes, I was being booked for a biopsy. Was I available in, say, an hour? Gina's reassurances evaporated in my mind. The red handkerchief unfolded before my eyes and there it was, the terror I had hidden for the past several days; the illusion was over. I called Grant and began to cry the minute he picked up the phone. He left his meeting and came straight to the hospital.

Lying on the table in a darkened room in the breast unit on the fifth floor of the cancer hospital, I didn't know for sure about the shift in nomenclature, from lump to tumour, but I had a fearful hunch. The walls of the examining room were bare; no artwork to distract me, no colour to brighten my thoughts. The biopsy technician wore a loose-knit beige sweater; a darker beige cotton shirt was visible through the holes of the open weave. Her manner was stern, cold and humourless—and those are the nice words I can say. Her stunning lack of empathy for a frightened young woman undergoing an urgent, spontaneous cancer test was without a doubt the low point in my medical care. Somehow the callous manner in which she removed the bloody probe from within the flesh of my bosom, indiscreetly passing it right in front of my eyes as if to antagonize the obvious pain and upset I was already feeling, made me even more glum about my prospects.

I had never had so much as a broken bone, merely three stitches—and those were laced into my finger in a doctor's office. My previously intact and functioning body was being poked—hard—by an ill-tempered clinician with the bedside manner of a cinderblock. This was never part of the plan.

———

MY HUSBAND AND I walked to the car in stunned confusion, huddled together against the cold wind and the fearful change swirling around us. On the drive home there was a construction crew jackhammering along part of our route, ripping open the concrete with fierce tools; I felt empathy for the road.

Stifling what I now know were rumblings of dread building in his gut, Grant reached out his right hand to me, palm facing up. This is our road-code for unity, a silent gesture of support shared on car trips. It is a peace offering in times of conflict, a loving extension of a joyous heart, or, as with any pair of held hands, a simple bond of connection. "We'll get through this, whatever happens," he said, his right arm still extended. "We can handle this. And I love you. I'll do anything I can for you."

I returned the gesture, placing my left hand palm down into his, though I said nothing in reply. My mind was, understandably, elsewhere. But I wasn't actually thinking about a cancer diagnosis. I was thinking about Jake. He and Sara were also leaving the hospital, probably right at that minute, just a block or two away.

After many heartbreaking years of failed pregnancies, with nothing but expense and anguish to show for their many attempts at the fertility clinic, my only sibling and his beloved bride were set to undergo their final round of in-vitro, putting the last two fertilized eggs into my sister-in-law, with all fingers and toes in the family obviously crossed for their fruition. This was their last hope. Their appointment had been scheduled for Monday, March 31, at 11:30 A.M.—the exact same day and time as my mammogram and ultrasound appointment, which had led immediately to the biopsy. While the entire family was on alert to direct all our powers of positive karma toward those two for this critical procedure, no one knew where I was or what I was undergoing at that time—it was too early in the game to worry anyone about my situation.

Needless to say I had dropped the ball on karmic channelling on their behalf that morning. By about 11:34 my left breast was having the life squeezed out of it in the panini press of the mammogram machine, followed by the cold ultrasound gel and looks of grave concern on the face of the technician. So I quite simply forgot to think of my sister-in-law and to send all my most loving, harmonious wishes for joy and happiness down the street to the fertility clinic where she was lying on a padded table of her own.

But just then, reaching for my husband's hand on the car ride home, I remembered how differently their morning had gone, how bright a light of hope was shining in their two hearts right now. They had delirious anticipation of good things to come; their results would be delivered in two weeks—as would mine.

I thought of the coincidence of our two medical experiences that day and chose to interpret that as significant. Nursing the tender bruise on my bandaged left breast, I conjured an image of the scales of justice teetering toward balance. On one side, an outspoken first-born sister with an abundance of good fortune, who gets pregnant—three times—just by thinking about it; on the other side, a gentle, soft-spoken younger brother with a giant heart and a million friends, trudging a wandering path to job satisfaction, aching desperately to be a father but thwarted in countless attempts.

Perhaps the real-life connection with Grant's warm hand in the face of hypothetical fear filled me with brash faith; I began a peculiar line of reasoning about where along life's curious path my brother and I now found ourselves. And so, along that slow-moving, noisy, construction-plagued ride home, I struck a bargain with the universe.

"Let me get breast cancer," I dared the Fates. "I'll take the hit. Let the bad news be mine this time, those two have had their share. If there can only be one good outcome to arise from these twinned sets of tenuous longing, give it to them."

I'm no martyr; I wasn't so melodramatic as to think I needed to die for my spirit to be reborn in my brother's child, for heaven's sake. But I knew breast cancer was something one could endure for a while and be done with, a bumpy twisting road that would eventually merge back onto the main highway. Childlessness was a more permanent condition. So I silently offered up my left breast, my hair, and the next year of my life so that those two could have a baby. The thought of me sidestepping misfortune synchronously as my brother suffered yet another of its blows was too nauseating to contemplate. I actually felt quite clever and sneaky about it all. I would get to live and hold my new little niece or nephew—two happy endings.

Looking back on that moment, I am galled by my own arrogance. Did I really presume to be able to control the narrative of not just my own fate, but my brother's as well?

the pull of nature

WHEN JAKE AND I were little, we spent our summers at the cottage on the Ottawa River. My father made the four-hour trek from the city to join us each weekend, but for all the other days of the long, lazy season we were alone with my mother. Most evenings after dinner she would take us out for a walk, exploring in the woods and on the public beach nearby. We had no destination, no purpose except to see what treasures the day had coughed up. Some nights we found puffballs, papery beige fungi that release a puff of spores when they burst. They were often found ruptured, but on a particularly fortuitous outing, we'd discover one wholly intact, and my mother would let us take turns squeezing the delicate shell and watching it wheeze a cloud of what looked like cigarette smoke. We found bird's eggs, mostly broken and empty; plenty of tiny brown toads that tickled the palm of your hand while you held them trapped. A double acorn hat was always a prized discovery, even more so if the acorns were still attached. It was on these walks that we sometimes spotted an isolated trillium. On the occasional evening when we did, my posy-loving mother would hold out her arms to make us stop and take a careful look at the trio of white petals hanging down, the arc of green leaves reaching up. We never saw more than one at a time; I always believed the trillium was a solitary flower. My mother told us, in reverential tones, that the trillium was rare and needed protection. It was, she said, against the law to dig one up. Jake and I became defenders, those nights, brave champions of the noble trillium. If anyone dared set foot on our island with the lonely flower's plunder on their mind, we felt ready for the fight.

Every so often we'd wake in the morning to see the waves on the river blowing the wrong way; then we knew we were in for what my mother called a Three Day Blow. The "wrong way" meant an east wind, when the wind blew against the river's westward current—a sure sign of bad weather. But I never minded a turn in the weather. The best weather of all was a thunderstorm. The way our family's small island is positioned, in one of the widest parts of the Ottawa River, you can see a storm travelling across the water toward you for several minutes before it arrives. Dark clouds begin to form as a backdrop to the distant Laurentian foothills; the dimmed light from the grey skies becomes flat. A day whose sparkling appearance was the equivalent of a glossy photo suddenly dons a matte finish as the first clue that a storm is on its way down the river. My mother is a cautious woman, never comfortable with undue risk, especially when it involved her young children. But there is no denying the magnetism of a summer storm, the best outdoor theatre of the season. After we had pulled the veranda furniture away from the screened windows so it wouldn't be damaged by the coming rain, she'd take us outside to the crest of the island's rocky slope to watch the show. Practical and tidy, yes she was, but not immune to the pull of nature. We would stand beneath a graceful pine and watch, the same spectacle every time. I can still feel the shift in the air as the temperature drops; hot summer haze becomes sharp and cool in a flash. Shadows darken the far hills, straight shafts of white angle down onto the distant forests of Quebec, plumes of rainfall. In the middle distance, islands upriver grow harder to make out, fading to a blur behind a low curb of silver fog as the rain pounds into the choppy water, spraying up a temper of mist. The river is a study in shades of slate grey. On the rock, we stand firm, though it's getting harder as the gust picks up. Small drops of rain begin to come; the wind hurls them at us, and they strike like fistfuls of gravel thrown by a bully. Now the islands across the river are invisible. A white scrim rolls across the water with steady determination—a fast-moving army of raindrops. The giant pine creaks as it sways in the wind, branches whipping above our heads. "It's coming for us!" Jake squeals, and grabs hold of my mother's leg. She is scared too, and soon she'll whisk us inside, but there's that delicious minute that I'm praying she'll let me stay for, when the full force of the storm strikes our shore and our bodies are battered by the winds and soaked in an instant and we are at the epicentre of nature, closer to its pulse than anything else on earth, and we are alive like we've never been before.

lesson number one

I HAD BEEN TOLD I'd have to wait seven to ten days for the biopsy results, so I wasn't expecting news until later in the week. But as soon as I stepped into the house after walking the boys to school, I sensed an odd flicker of energy that told me something was wrong. I heard the click of our cordless phone being hung up (who would be calling at nine o'clock sharp?), which meant my husband had not yet left for work (why was he still here?). Silence for a beat or two (why didn't he call out a greeting to me?). Standing in the back hall, in a moment now weirdly elongated in my memory, the seconds reverberated with what felt like a turning point. As Grant walked toward the door, I could almost mouth the words along with him as he spoke. "That was the doctor's office. She wants you to come in to meet with her at one o'clock to discuss the results of your biopsy. She said I should come too."

We sat for a long time in our hushed space. Grant and I are almost never alone in our house, especially during the day. I looked around the room at every piece of art we had bought and hung together, at the red and blue hockey gloves our boys had failed to put away before school, at the open

CD cases, shelves lined with books: evidence of all the life that goes on in this house. At this moment it all felt terribly muted and still, as if a pause button had been pressed on the whirring, joyous pandemonium of our time together. We held each other on the couch, crying quietly.

Eventually, we turned our thoughts to the practical realities of a one o'clock appointment, most notably Miles, who finished school at eleven-thirty. We would need to get him a babysitter. Telling my mother was out of the question, too much potential stress to add to the situation before we'd had time to process it ourselves. All our regular teenage babysitters would be at school in the middle of the day. We realized we'd have to resort to June, the fairly odd twenty-something babysitter we didn't use very often. Naturally, we couldn't tell her why we were booking her on such short notice; we'd just say I had a last-minute appointment.

I have no recollection of picking Miles up from school, no memory of the walk home. What did we talk about? Did we hold hands as usual? My brain is dark, a typical symptom of shock. I must have explained to him that Mama had to go out for a little while and that June would be arriving shortly to play with him. And what an arrival she made.

Into my chemical-free, microwave-free house where homemade organic food is stored in glass containers to avoid any contact with the dubious chemicals in plastic, burst the babysitter.

"Hey I'm sorry I'm late, you know? I have just had the worst possible week. My boyfriend's father was just diagnosed with cancer—I mean, cancer can you believe it? I just packed him into the ambulance for his tracheotomy. Listen is it okay if I brought us some lunch? I made some

Kraft Dinner, you know the real kind with that extra neon-orangey cheese, not that organic stuff you buy. Won't that be awesome, Miles? I made it last night in the microwave." And with that she pulled out a large plastic tub of microwaved neon-orange macaroni.

I remained mute, surrendering to the chemical assault on my child, and pulled on my coat to leave. June continued to catalogue all the tragic complexities of her father-in-law's cancer, including how it was tearing the family apart and causing her boyfriend to lose so much sleep he thought he might lose his job. I found myself almost happy to be going to the doctor's office to be told I had cancer, just so I could get out of the house.

———

TWO HOURS LATER we returned. My head was pounding; every muscle felt weak. My entire being held in the clutch of fear and confusion. Before I could put on a brave face for my kids, I was blasted by a toxic funk. As Grant ran around opening every window and door for fresh air (on this frigid day), June explained that she and Miles had bought some plasticine at the dollar store (Made in China! Out of who knows what!) and painted it with glow-in-the-dark nail polish for added sparkle effect. After several more minutes of elaborating on the challenges of dealing with a cancer diagnosis, she finally sailed out the door.

I am two hours into being a cancer patient. Lesson Number One: surrender control.

broken

Yours is the deepest hole, cancer. You have repossessed and forever tainted the letter C. You sneak up on smooth-running operations and overwhelm the system, splintering forms, families, futures. A shiny black jacket conceals your cavernous bowel; dark glasses hide your hollow eyes, sockets of brow bone. You are crepuscular emptiness, the consummate menace; you will never know love. Cruising with a villainous strut, you command submission; we bow in your presence.

The cancer diagnosis shoves a girl onto the dance floor under one of those flashing mirrored disco balls. Quivers of bright light interrupt the darkness. No matter how freely she tries to move through space, she appears to be lurching from one random, uncomfortable pose to the next; flashes of awkward form. She is surrounded by faces, colours, stores of cognitive data too many and too fast-moving to process effectively. The pace is frantic, like the beat of the disco melody (*Gloria! Gloria! I think they got your number* ...). She feels the music and does her best to make graceful motion to keep up with the beat, but to those watching at the dance floor's edge, the scene is just a blur, a catastrophe of motion, her carriage ultimately inscrutable, her body a sequence of disconnected positions.

Why did this happen to me? I measured carbon emissions, rode my bike in the rain, said no to high fructose corn syrup and yes to rabbit food. I tried everything I could to fix what seemed to be wrong, so how could it be me that winds up broken?

Windows had been shuttered, every latch bolted against harm. I thought I had everything under control. What did I miss? Where was the crack in the mortar, the fissure that let cancer in? My head hung in fool's shame, chastened for having thought I could dodge disaster. Every junk-food eating, SUV-driving detractor loomed in my vision, jeering my failure, mocking my vain attempts at control. Voices punished me at night, waking me from sleep to ridicule every sacrifice I had made for my health, for the earth. How could I have thought I might save the planet when I couldn't even keep myself safe from harm?

I am damp at first light, sweat-soaked after a night of fitful sleep. Nothing makes sense. I dream I am an English major who has boned up, verse and line, on post-colonial literature only to arrive at the examination hall and find the test is on the electromagnetic spectrum of binary stars. I do not understand astrophysics. I do not understand why I am here. *Where is the English faculty's exam hall? Where can I write out my treatise on* Wide Sargasso Sea? *Where can I go to prove to you that I did my homework, studied hard, know the answers?* My muffled dream-squawks echo, unanswered.

How did this happen? I thought I was prepared, but I never saw this coming.

THE WIGGLY PURPLE plastic salamander in Miles's loot bag is toxic, and I'm not sure what to do about it. He's wired on high-fructose corn syrup and maltodextrin, the two main ingredients in the bright blue icing on a Pac-Man birthday cake. He spent the past two hours eating genetically modified cornmeal (Cheezies) and reconstituted pig innards (hot dogs), spirits racing accordingly. So he may fly off the handle if I mention that the nifty cheap plastic reptile he has gleefully acquired is made from toxic petrochemicals that could cause reproductive damage to his future procreative self and that he'd better put it straight into the garbage and wash his hands carefully. Or if I point out the flaws in the Made-in-China dollar-store model of offshore production of cheap crap that spews greenhouse gas emissions while being transported halfway around the world only to end up in a landfill site when it breaks after a few days' use.

There was a time when I would have engaged in this battle without hesitation; but today, I am silent. I wish I didn't know everything that's wrong with this otherwise simple childhood moment, and I wish I didn't care.

———

MY HUSBAND TAKES ME out for dinner, to talk, react, process. Seeking solace and pleasure in the face of fear, we order too many of our favourite dishes at the south Indian restaurant. Awash in fitful conjecture, we find comfort in the predictability of the familiar menu. Over aloo gobi and saag paneer, we think of questions we must ask the doctors; over eggplant bharta and chana masala we speculate about possible treatment schedules; over pulao rice and onion pakoras we mull the mystery of how the picture of our life and my health came to look like this. We gnaw on that one like a massive chunk of gristle, trying to break it open, figure it out. But it cannot be digested. The Why question remains, unanswered. Unanswerable.

Two hours later, mounds of uneaten food remain on the table; frustration and fear have had their way with my appetite. Amidst our profuse apologies, the waiter clears our leftovers and returns moments later with two plastic takeout bags, each containing a stack of Styrofoam containers: towers of unsustainability. Instinctively I wince at the waste; avoiding any contribution to landfill is a reflexive habit. But then I catch myself worrying about harming the earth with my dinner wrappers, and it somehow feels ridiculous. Like wiping the countertops before the tsunami hits. I take a bag and head for the door.

the weight of the world

IDID WONDER, that sleet-filled day in early April when I learned that one half of the deal had come to pass, whether the Fates had actually agreed to my cockamamie reverse-Faustian bargain. Did this mean Jake and Sara would soon become parents? Actually the only thing that kept my spirits up in those few heart-in-my-mouth days before I told anyone in my family, was thinking that my shamefully control-minded plot might have worked, envisioning my brother's elated phone call as the antidote to our gloom. I pictured the parallel trajectories of our experiences, linked only by our matching start lines; she would blossom and grow more rosy and full of promise, while I had every whisper of threat removed from me. I pictured the happy day we would welcome the newest member of the Deacon family. I wondered how cute that baby would look when we first met. I wondered, too, how I would look.

So their heartbroken phone call was a double blow, as was my news to them when I visited them later.

I had said I wanted to come over to their house, to commiserate in person. Grant stayed home with the boys so that I could bear this conversation alone. When I arrived at my brother's, we embraced, wordless; there was little left to say about their doleful state that hadn't been said countless times already over the past three years. The soaring heights of hope and the crashing depths of despair had become hideously routine; the cruel and costly cycle of infertility that kept landing them back into this familiar pit of thick, black mud, sucking and yanking with almighty force every time they tried to step out.

For several moments we sat quietly in Jake and Sara's living room. As I considered how best to interrupt the course of this particular melancholy by unloading my own shitty news, my fingers and palms grew damp in spite of the cool April weather; I smoothed the cream-coloured cotton of their chesterfield repeatedly. After a few minutes my heart was pounding so hard I began to shiver. *More bad news, I'm afraid.* I blurted it out. *Breast cancer. MRI next week. Surgery next month.* No tears, no melodrama, just the frightening secret I had held back from my dearest family members for several days, crashing out of my mouth like boulders from a dump truck.

For just a minute as Jake and Sara processed this new grief that was not their own, I felt strangely peaceful, buoyed up by the power of one devastating diagnosis to relieve the sting of another. I took some small comfort in being a distraction from their suffering. But the effect was temporary. We said goodbye, parted with swaying embraces and promises to talk the next day. On the way out to my car, the tears came on like a downpour.

On the drive home, my sinuses were swollen like a spring creek, awash in emotional mucus. I pulled over to blow my nose and clear my vision. A bright pink sign on the storefront out the window lit up the darkened sidewalk beside the car. "Manicure, Pedicure, No Appointment Necessary." Another nail bar opening up; another team of underpaid aestheticians, inhaling toxic chemical fumes all day through flimsy paper masks. Why don't they have cancer?

I reached into the back seat for my purse. Every mother carries tissues in her purse; I, need I tell you, carry a reusable linen handkerchief. Among other things. My husband marvels on a regular basis at the weight of my shoulder bag. It takes two hands to lift it up and over the seat, a workout for the rotator cuff.

I sifted through the contents of my purse, looking for my handkerchief. Dental floss. Lip balm (beeswax!). Makeup kit. Reading glasses. Hand sanitizer (organic! triclosan-free!). Safety pin. Comb. Magnifying glass. Wallet. Paperclips. Swiss Army knife. Reusable cloth grocery bags (four). Keys. Notebook. Pens (two). Handkerchief, at last.

The emergency flasher lights blinked an excuse for my roadside breakdown. As my sinuses began to settle into a calmer state, it occurred to me that some people depart for overnight camping trips with less paraphernalia than I carry on my shoulder for a trip to the bank. My purse embodies my best attempts at control; it is a portable force field against chaos. Flaxseed caught in molars before job interview? I've got toothpicks. Sudden onset of hay fever? Handkerchief at the ready. Spontaneous picnic? I can provide slicing and cork-pulling services. When I pulled a miniature measuring tape out of a Christmas cracker at last year's holiday dinner, I relished the notion of adding it to the weighty collection on my shoulder. Like my mother before me, I want to be ready for whatever situation might arise. I want to have the solution, to stave off the relative anguish of botched circumstances.

Why does a woman carry the weight of the world in her purse? To maintain control under whatever circumstance may arise. We take curious pride in near-universal preparation. I may not be able to set a fractured tibia or patch a leak on the Space Shuttle, but in more quotidian conundrums, I am often able to provide rescue by extracting the necessary item from my handbag. Producing an on-the-spot solution to a simple dilemma brings untold rewards: the solution of the problem, yes, but what's more, the glorious pride at having anticipated the course of events and invested the forethought and effort that will resolve it. The daily weight of so many often-unused items pales in comparison to the lightness of being when we can smooth a wrinkled situation simply by digging into our purse. My desire to control outcomes outweighs my desire for everyday physical comfort. By about ten pounds.

With the one dry corner of my handkerchief, I wiped the last teardrops from my eyelashes, then dropped the soggy cloth back into my purse. The last glow of saved daylight on this cool spring evening had faded, surrendering to darkness altogether. Now it was real. My brother knew I had cancer, which meant I really had cancer. Which meant I had to tell everyone else.

If I have cancer, I am mortal, flawed, vulnerable, weak. Wrong. I must have done something wrong. Cancer is the ultimate failure, an inability to repel doom. When people find out I have cancer, they will see that I have failed. That I didn't have the right information, that my lifestyle wasn't an antidote to misfortune—that there was no Secret Path.

My carefully planned sequence of steps has led me ... to the edge of a cliff.

We play a game on the river in the summertime, an old lumberjack's challenge to see who can balance for the longest time on a rolling log in deep water.

The log is mighty, two feet across and fifteen feet long, its thick bark the colour of mud mixed with charcoal. Floating in the river it becomes soaked, the hard nubby chunks of raised bark grow soggy, the divots and crevices fill with water. There are usually one or two bare patches along the trunk where bark has fallen off, showing golden brown flesh of wood beneath. The patches quickly become slippery, coated with a film of gel—treacherous for the fast-stepping log roller.

Someone steadies the log until both rollers have successfully mounted their chosen ends, and then lets go. At that moment the pace and motion of the giant felled tree become the sole doing of the two log rollers, trying to control the rotation of the trunk with their feet, trying to stay aloft as the spin quickens.

The roller's feet scurry to keep ahead of the rotations, flitting forward and backward like an Irish dancer, top speed. Quick steps, small and light, carefully placed, eyes on the bark, dodging the bare patches as they spin by. Then the competitor on the other end of the giant trunk shifts hard and the pace slows until the log spins in reverse. Now it speeds up again running the other way, water streaming through the deep channels in the bark, a swirling circular fall. A quick shuffle of the feet and the roller has turned around so her feet still run forward.

This is how I have lived my life, moving at top speed to stay on top of what comes, checking the pace, direction, anticipating next steps to stay upright.

But then the competitor shifts direction again, and our log roller loses focus. The slightest miscalculation of pace and rotation leads to a misstep. A foot lands on the gooey open wood. She slips, arms whirlwind backward, clinging desperately to the vestiges of balance. But it is gone. And the roller falls, lands in the black river. Cold, submerged; through the murky waters she can see the rings on the log's end, still spinning slowly after her fall.

I turn off the emergency flashers, restart the engine, and heave the satchel of readiness onto the front seat, making a mental note to purge some of its weight when I get home. Right now its ambitions seem futile.

conviction escapes me

M Y DOWNWARD DOG collapsed today. In the upside-down V pose I have been holding for months at yoga practice, the body's weight is evenly distributed between the arms and the legs. My legs are like tanks, they could hold anything forever, but I have the arm strength of a sickly nine-year-old. It takes my full concentration to conjure the might to hold up my body in that pose, and today it escaped me. Instead of focusing on being strong and breathing through the discomfort of the pose, I fixated on having cancer. I thought about being sick, which made me feel weak, which made me collapse. Already I can't seem to focus on my children, on my responsibilities as a mother. My patience has evaporated. I worry that I am becoming emotionally and physically absent from them; in learning to let go, cut myself slack, and lower the pressure on myself, I'm handing more and more parenting and domestic responsibility off to other people. A voice in my head suggests that this is the beginning of phasing myself out of my children's lives, preparing them for a life without me.

Grant joined us on the walk to school this morning, something quite outside our normal routine. The walk to school, complete with hand-holding and discussions about the day ahead, is usually my bailiwick. It is one of the few times in the day when I feel focused on my kids; the other time is when I read them a bedtime story. No meals to cook, chores to oversee, phone calls to answer, or work to attend to, just time together with my boys. My sporty husband is forever playing soccer in the park with them, or a backyard game of hoops. They watch hockey together, play hockey together, discuss hockey together, read the sports section together. But for bedtime stories and the walks to and from school, I'm their gal. These are the moments when my disinclination for team sports matters not.

This morning, though, their father joined us on the walk to school, and you would think for all the world that he'd been on the other side of the earth for the past six weeks. They clung to him as to a life raft, they joked and laughed with him as with a best friend. I fell behind them on the crowded sidewalk and watched, as they ambled ahead, the posse of men in my life. They seemed completely self-sufficient—a loving, capable father and his three doting, sporty sons. It gave me both comfort and grief to think that they would be completely fine without me.

———

LATER, WALKING TOWARD the grocery store, I bump into a friend. News of my diagnosis brews on my tongue; I steel myself against any judgment that may accompany her pity. But before I can even begin a conversation and reveal my bad news, she leaps into a tirade of self-flagellation, apologizing for carrying plastic bags. "I thought I was only coming to the store for one thing but I ended up buying more. I forgot my cloth bags at home, I swear. I almost always have them with me, I can't believe I'm running into you on the one day I forgot them!"

Now it is she who steels herself against what she expects will be my judgment. I'm the Planetary Watchdog, it seems, ready to pounce with earth-minded opinion. A friend once told me that his teenage son brought my *Green for Life* book on the car trip to the cottage and read aloud the entire way, informing his family of best practices they needed to implement to shrink their footprint. He said they spent their entire weekend debating the ecological pros and cons of hand-washing versus machine-washing the dishes, discussing the merits of cedar over pressure-treated wood for the dock. The family mantra for their cottage weekend became, *"What would Gill Deacon do?"* The great know-it-all—if something is wrong with the environment, Gill will tell you how to fix it. The funny thing is, I hadn't even noticed my friend's plastic grocery bags. Yet I'm guilty by association, aligned forever-more with sensible, prudent earth-friendly choices.

I'm not sure I want the job anymore.

That toe-tingling conviction escapes me; my limbs are numb. I don't know if I have the right to tell anyone else to live the way I do. I certainly can't tell them it's an inoculation against the mind-warping terror of a cancer diagnosis.

I wonder about the arrogance required to try to steer human behaviour and effect change. Did I think I was invulnerable and that I really had all the answers? Cancer is a slap in the face to invincibility. It is the skull parked incongruously amidst the subjects in an oil painting, intimation of certain death. It is the slave, marching one short step behind the ancient Roman general who once led a victory parade through the streets of Rome, whispering in the general's ear over the din of the cheering crowds, *"Memento mori."* *Remember that you, too, will die.*

How busy, loud, distracted I have been while trying to lead the parade. I had never stopped the protest march long enough to hear that old Latin message. But now I feel the skull's weight, perched on my shoulder.

psychological resilience

ELLING MY CHILDREN turned out to be a multi-step process, involving many conversations of varying degrees of intensity depending on the child, spread over several days as the information settled in.

For the initial announcement, Grant and I gathered the boys around the dining room table for a powwow. At first, they assembled with customary distraction and fraternal skirmishes over who got to hold which action figure. Something quickly stilled them, though, to a silent rapt attention not seen before or since in our testosterone-filled home. Perhaps they intuited a problem, could see through our best but likely vain attempts to balance sobriety with confidence.

"Mama has cancer," Grant said. The C word, always a show-stopper. Funny how even young, healthy children understand the razor-sharp impact of that diagnosis, feel the ten-ton weight of those two simple syllables.

Reggie's responsible first-born eyes filled with tears. Miles put down his Darth Vader Lego, as though suddenly repelled by its childishness. Harper was the first to speak.

"Is it the dying kind?"

A beat of silence as Grant and I glanced at each other, unsure of the exact placement of our next foot along the high wire.

"Probably not," one of us said.

Harper seemed immediately satisfied that all would be well. He began to jiggle his legs, anxious to get back onto his skateboard.

Grant and I tried to walk the impossible tightrope between telling the truth about the dreadful, invisible player that had taken a seat at our family table and instilling reassurance that we could handle it; serve up what it was asking for, then send it on its way.

We told them we didn't know exactly what our life would look like over the next while, or how long that while might last, but that we thought in the end everything would be all right. And that we would let them know if any of that information were to change.

We kept it short, not wanting to burden their small shoulders with any more weight than was necessary, hoping to somehow salvage the safe, united, harmonious world we had tried to create for our brood up to this point, in which their parents had reasonably satisfactory answers to most questions and were not themselves vulnerable.

I contemplated the speech to my parents a hundred times, wondering how to share the news of my not-so-Just-So diagnosis. My father's mother had died of breast cancer. The only time I ever saw him cry was when he heard the news of her passing. Perched on a rock by the shore of the mighty Ottawa, he looked smaller than I'd ever thought of him; his back slumped in uncharacteristic weakness. I still remember how he wept. How do you relate news of calamitous uncertainty to someone devoted to order and harmony? What kind of failing grade does a cancer diagnosis receive, with so much room for improvement? Is there a right way to send someone you love down the dark corridor of worry, to visit with the spectres of anguish, of disfigurement, of loss? How can any parent help but assume a degree of responsibility, however misplaced, for some unseen error in the past, a dropped thread of maternal care that lead to their child's eventual suffering? And how can a child programmed to meet expectations deliver news of such jarring discord? Details were relayed selectively. *Cancer, left breast, 2.2 cm* I told them; *locally advanced, aggressive, invasive* I did not. Parking all fear, I regaled them with *top-notch doctors,* and *excellent survival rates. Just a lump and a bump in the road.* I said that I would be all right—what else could I tell them? And I resolved to make it so. My mother cried silently on the other end of the phone; my father said he was sorry and that he was sure I'd be all right. His voice sounded smaller than usual.

The next day, my mother arrived with some flowers and a warm embrace. She wore a necklace of bright silver that matched the colour of her hair. Her energy was much more upbeat than I had anticipated; I suspect she was working pretty hard at it. She said she had read in a magazine that a good attitude would help with my recovery. "Psychological resilience" I think she called it: the ability to stay focused on the bright side, to dwell on the meaningful things and not the pesky details. She'd read that just believing you would get well would help you get well; attitude over circumstance— sounded like a classic Oprah maxim. (Oprah is another of my mother's mainstays for advice, mostly salubrious.)

Probing further, I found that in fact the notion of staving off regression or recurrence with an upbeat disposition is axiomatic within breast cancer circles. Positive thinking is its own kind of adjuvant therapy. Which meant there was a right way to have cancer. Cancer didn't have to be a death sentence—and let's face it, in this day and age, breast cancer seldom is. Instead, it might just be the newest challenge to be met, survival just one more thing to achieve. And with that, I shifted from being crushed by cancer to resolving to be good at it. This was familiar territory: an assignment where I'm judged on my performance. While I would never have chosen the part, it became a role I could rally to. Ace my cancer.

room for improvement

Subject: mri results are in
Attachment: photograph of me wearing a pale blue hospital
gown and a pair of knee-high Frye boots, striking a *Saturday
Night Fever* disco pose

so this is me last thursday trying to pretend i wasn't super
freaked out about sliding face down into a tube for 40 minutes
with my hands strapped behind my back. actually, i just thought
the mri outfit went quite nicely with my boots.
i did survive, obviously, though not without the help of a couple
of sedatives. (note to self for future mri's—take the sedatives
more than 20 minutes before sliding into the tube so that they
relax you DURING the mri, not AFTER the mri when you're at a
family wine tasting event. oops.)
anyway, the mri was important as it was the final word on the
size, shape, dimensions, location, and spread of my little bump.
knowing that helps determine the treatment, which in turn tells
me what my summer will look like!
so the good news is that the mri results were the best we could
have hoped for.
actually, i suppose the best results we could have hoped for

would have been, "oh would you look at that, it appears you swallowed a raisin that went down the wrong way, what a funny place for it to end up!"

but second to that, the best results would have been that the breast cancer is:

#1 localized (meaning it hasn't started moving around the breast)

#2 not in the lymph nodes (not a definitive diagnosis, only surgery can tell for sure, but it's a really good sign)

#3 not in the other breast.

and that's what we got! three for three, woohoo!

MOVING ON FROM those first days of stunned gloom about my diagnosis, I roared into problem-solving mode. Upbeat stubborn determination was my modus operandi, in emails to family and friends, and in my cancer-fighting research mission. I hit the bookstore and the library, tottering home under a pile of cancer books. *Cancer Is a Word, Not a Sentence*; *Natural Strategies for Cancer Patients*; *Anticancer*; *Crazy Sexy Cancer*; *Outsmart Your Cancer*; *Hope in the Face of Cancer*... Half of them I returned, unread; the voice or the message didn't resonate. I wanted ingenuity, needed to learn how to think outside the medical box, but I didn't want to have to turn my life upside down and become a cultish freak, eating nothing but raw zucchini. As a vegetarian with allergies to wheat, cow's milk, and sugar, I already feel like a freak. Try having me over for dinner, you'll see what I mean.

I sought answers from trusted professionals, even beyond the hospital doors. Homeopaths, nutritionists, immunologists—I consulted them all, at my own expense. Usually, it feels like money well spent, but the alternative route to health is also lined with money magnets that can leave you more confused than you started out.

Nancy had been recommended by a trusted friend not long after my diagnosis. I was desperate to take some of my care into my own hands; I couldn't operate a surgical scalpel or a chemo drip, but I knew I could make myself feel better with food. Diet and nutrition were already part of my environmental repertoire. A breathless devotee of Michael Pollan (so enormous is my regard for the sustainable and healthy food author of *In Defense of Food* and *The Omnivore's Dilemma*, I once choked on my local, organic mesclun greens when he sat down across the table from me at an event, and proceeded to twist my hair and giggle vacuously throughout the rest of the meal, much as I would have had Shaun Cassidy joined me at lunch in the mid-1970s), I considered myself a fairly healthy eater. I had the "Eat food—Not too much—Mostly plants" mantra committed to memory; I seasoned with fresh-picked herbs from my garden; I knew a collard from a rutabaga and had recipes for both. But there was room for improvement. *Foods that Fight Cancer*, by Richard Béliveau, was by this time a bestseller; I wanted to bolster my nutritional efforts any way I could.

"Nancy's a holistic nutritionist, I think you'll really like her. She specializes in cancer diagnoses," my friend advised.

I didn't ask what a holistic nutritionist was. I have a healthy appetite for lateral thinking; I figured I'd give her a try.

I made the long trek to Nancy's suburban office, jittery

with eager anticipation—taking the cancer battle into my own hands, how empowering! She greeted me at the door, wearing a smart grey pencil skirt with a matching jacket. She was tall, thin, with shoulder length brown hair. I guessed she was in her late forties. She looked slightly wan, like she could use a sandwich. Nancy ushered me into a comfortable padded chair across the dark wooden desk from where she sat, and began to explain her philosophy.

"Cancer is caused by four things, Gillian. Do you know what they are?"

I began to rack my brain for a response. Smoking? Asbestos?

"The doctors won't tell you this, but it's absolutely proven. The causes of cancer are easy to remember with the acronym TAPE: Toxins, Acids, Parasites, and Emotion."

Wooh, boy. I shifted gears. We were out on the fringes, here. Must remember that. Just listen and observe, save judgment for later.

"Most people don't have sufficient fibre in their diet to eliminate toxins on a regular basis," Nancy went on. "If the diet is ideal, what you eat today, you should poop tomorrow. I'd like to see you have three to four poops a day."

I assumed she didn't really mean she'd like to *see* me having all those poops; I was hoping a report would suffice.

"The other dietary factor that leads to cancer is too much acidity. You'll need to start thinking about your environment." I had thought for so long about *the* environment; now it was time to think about mine.

"Cancer cannot survive in an alkaline environment. Most of the modern Western diet is highly acidic: bagels, dough-nuts, meat, dairy products. Acidity in the digestive system means food doesn't get broken down properly, which means it gets stored in the intestines and turns toxic."

My cellphone rang in the middle of her digestion speech; I apologized for having forgotten to turn off the ringer, then answered. It was the cancer hospital calling to inform me of my MRI booking the following week. I repeated the directions aloud as I jotted them down (waiting area B, third floor, nothing to eat or drink for eight hours prior ...) then hung up, turning back to the desk.

Nancy was looking at me with a mixture of empathy and disgust. "You know, I'm not legally allowed to tell you that you should not go ahead with medical cancer treatment, but I have to tell you that your cancer can be controlled and completely eradicated with diet."

Eradicated? Without painful medical interventions? What kind of diet could do that?

"A raw diet," Nancy said. "I would like you to alter your diet significantly to improve your immune system and digestion."

I should pause here to mention that there are many people on this earth who might consider me a hard-core health nut. I don't eat bagels or doughnuts or meat. My pantry is full of chickpeas and quinoa; my vegetable drawers bulge with collards and cabbage. I have bee pollen in my refrigerator.

But Nancy suggested I ramp it up a bit and stop killing all those digestive enzymes by heating my food to over 150 degrees Celsius. She suggested I eat 80 percent raw food and become entirely vegan. No eggs, no dairy.

I had heard about detox treatment centres where cancer patients go for a last-gasp shot at beating the disease, where raw food and round-the-clock juicing were the ticket to restoring health; tumours that had been unassailable in the face of devastating chemotherapy shrank down to nothing.

All right, I thought, maybe I could see my way to incorporating more raw food into my diet.

"Oh," Nancy added, "and definitely no wine. Way too acidic. The only thing I'd like to see you drinking every day is two glasses of freshly juiced vegetables." Sweet Jesus.

Nancy laid out a goal and promised reward if I reached it. Her exacting nutritional regimen set a higher standard for mastering this experience—crack cocaine to a first-born. I needed to be good at having cancer, so I bought in. Not all the way; I had no intention of choosing to get rid of my tumour with raw mustard greens *instead of* surgery (how could I explain that to my boys?), but I wanted to have a hand in my own recovery, administrate at least some part of my own treatment. Eating right—really right—seemed like a good, if challenging, first step.

As I pulled up later in front of my house, I waved to Margaret, an elderly neighbour who was passing by with her dog. Stepping out of the car, I asked after her family, in a perfunctory, unloading-the-groceries-while-we-chat kind of way, anxious to get my bags of raw vegetables into the house and begin noshing. Margaret's chin began to quiver as she explained that her thirty-one-year-old niece had just died of breast cancer. Shit. Why do people tell me this stuff? I put down my cloth bag, overflowing with spinach. "She beat it the first time, but then it came back a few years later, more aggressive than ever." Margaret could not possibly know how her words were changing the course of my day, my nightmares, even as she uttered them. But then she laced the bitter pill with a sweet reprieve: "But she always had such a terrible diet, ever since she was a girl. Don't know if that had anything to do with it ..." And there it was, the invitation to control an outcome. Margaret's niece must not have known what I now knew from Nancy. She mustn't have mustered enough discipline over her appetites. I can will myself to manage the outcome of my cancer through diet, I reasoned. There on the sidewalk, holding a week's worth of green vegetables that I intended to eat before sundown, that became the window of hope to leap through: an escape from the burning building.

As if to prove a point, my friend Debbie dropped by that afternoon bearing a thoughtful, if unusual, gift: a small plastic bag filled with a phallic root. It was beige, blistered, and ugly, like a Tolkien finger—a sure sign it must be good for me.

"Turmeric, an excellent cancer-fighter," she explained, having kindly undertaken research on the matter. Like the yellow powder in my spice drawer? "Yeah, but it's better if you eat it raw, straight from the root." Of course it is.

———

MY VISIT WITH NANCY marked the beginning of a new approach to being a cancer patient. Control *was* still an option, I had discovered. But it would require extraordinary effort to manage my cancer outcome, to make it Just So. The first hour of every morning is a testament to my madness. Rising from sleep to a bleating alarm, I shuffle down the hallway to the bathroom. I sit on the toilet to empty the overnight contents of my bladder. Midway through the stream, on days when I am alert enough to remember, I stop it. After birthing three large-headed boys, arresting one's pee stream is a Herculean feat, requiring significant muscle contraction and more than a little concentration. At this hour of the morning, neither of those can be counted on. A critical imperative snaps me alert: I need to test my urine to establish the pH levels, to see how alkaline my system is. Cancer, Nancy's voice echoed in my ears, cannot survive in an alkaline environment.

Reaching up to the shelf above the sink, I grab the small yellow roll of pH testing paper, tear off a thumb-length section, and grasp it in between my legs. The stream of urine resumes (blessedly), darkening the yellow paper. I remove the soaking strip, trying not to let it drip pigmented pee onto my legs, the floor, my pyjamas. Holding the limp, wet paper over the sink with one hand, my rear end still hovering over the toilet bowl, pyjama bottoms curled around my ankles on the cold tile floor, I grab the pH test dispenser with the other hand. It is marked with ten small stripes in various shades: golden yellow, chartreuse, darker citrine yellow, a selection of greens from summer grass to olivaceous mud. Lining my dripping sample up against the colour-coded package, I squint my barely awake eyes to see which hue my test strip most closely resembles. The darker the paper, the better; light coloration means acidic urine, darker suggests a more alkaline system. On the swamp-green days I breathe a sigh of relief, gloating to the empty bathroom about my urinary accomplishment; on lemon-yellow days I wince, mentally kick myself for not eating enough dark, leafy, alkaline-forming vegetables, vowing to juice more raw collard greens before day's end. I make a mental note of the corresponding number that accompanies that morning's colour and determine to write it down when I get to my desk after breakfast. Occasionally I actually remember.

After depositing the soggy paper into the wastebasket, I complete my bathroom ablutions (including a good hand wash) and make my way downstairs to the kitchen. I let the dog out in the backyard. Watching him crouch his haunches on the beleaguered grass, I envy the simplicity of his morning pee: no testing, no measuring, just sweet release. He shakes, sniffs around a little, then comes back inside to keep me company.

Most of my family is still asleep. Occasionally, my husband will have risen early to finish a work assignment or to get a head start on the sports section before he has to do battle for it with one or more of our boys. On those lucky mornings when I find him here, we embrace, offering cursory concern for each other's night of rest. He will have put on the kettle, his only morning thought being an urgent desire for coffee. I admire the straightforwardness of his morning habits: coffee, newspaper, poop, shower, work. Lucky guy.

Taking a deep breath, I assiduously knuckle down to my own, more ridiculous morning regimen. If cancer is a battle waged by the immune system, I'm doing everything I can to fortify the troops.

Freshly squeezed organic lemon in hot water (good for the kidneys, immune booster). Wait twenty minutes for maximum digestion.

Use twenty minutes wisely, preparing world's most complicated breakfast. Each step is choreographed, with the efficient, precision movement of a Bob Fosse routine, only fewer sequins.

Poach egg, preferably organic. Organic eggs have higher levels of omega-3 fatty acids, vitamin B, and folic acid. And besides, who wants stylish clothing or a European vacation? Organic food is so much more fun to spend all your money on.

Assemble bowl of cereal: homemade raw granola (no sugar!), ground flaxseeds (lowers cholesterol!), ground chia seeds (stabilizes blood sugar!), drizzle of flax oil (builds cell membranes, kills cancer cells!), sheep's milk yogourt (less lactose, easier to digest!), fresh blueberries, raspberries, strawberries, and blackberries (cancer-fighting antioxidants!), vitamin D drops on top (must be taken with protein!). The refrigerator door opens and closes with the flurry of a bedroom farce. I have been awake for possibly eight minutes and already I am perspiring, racing against the clock to tackle every potential health challenge before my hungry schoolboys come downstairs and set the wheels of modern family chaos into motion. One spoonful of protein powder, one of dehydrated greens. Add juice for flavour, water to thin the muck. Mix and stir concoction until it resembles swamp water. Set aside.

And now for the icing on the cake, the ultimate rigmarole: the vitamin brigade.

Selenium, one with breakfast. Alpha lipoic acid, antioxidant booster. Vitamin C, immune system kick. Biotin, can't remember why. Vitamin B, two yellow hornets. Calcium, horse pill. Magnesium, three sleek, elegant bullets. Vitamin E, glistening gel cap the size of a USB stick. Vitamin K, two with fat. Essential fatty acids, must be kept cold. Acidophilus, for healthy digestion. Multivitamin, for active women. Oh, I'm active all right, lifting all these kegs of health pellets.

Two dozen pills pop into my mouth at every meal, a constellation of shapes and colours. I fill a small white-lidded tub with this colourful cornucopia of supplements, bring it with me to the table. I throw them back, one by one, with a chaser of swamp water. Yellow ones, brown ones, tiny discs, a hulking bolus.

———

THE JUICER IN WHICH I invested a small fortune looks not unlike a sturdy, robotic aardvark. A ridged, white, hard plastic bulge houses the "magnetic and bio-ceramic technology": twin metal rotating gears that could extract liquid from a paperweight. The gaping maw of a feed tube reaches skyward, gobbling stalks, stems, pulp, and peel with equal eagerness; a squat tongue spits out the unwanted remains—automatic pulp ejection, baby. The highly coveted Exposed Pulp Adjustment knob is the nose of our aardvark, and, I'm told, one of the reasons this thing cost so damn much money. One might reasonably purchase a second-hand car for less money than I spent on my juicer.

The desiccator of all things raw and juiceable is a rite of passage, it seems, for the modern-day cancer patient, certainly for those who have had a visit with Nancy, or who have read one of her recommended books, *The pH Miracle*, by Dr. Robert O. Young. In it, Dr. Young writes, "The pH level of our internal fluids affects every cell in our bodies. The entire metabolic process depends on an alkaline environment. Chronic overacidity corrodes body tissue, and if left unchecked will interrupt all cellular activities and functions, from the beating of your heart to the neural firing of your brain. In other words, overacidity interferes with life itself."

To achieve the ideal pH state of alkalinity, all anti-cancer nutrition bibles advise that Thou Shalt Drink Two Glasses of Juiced Vegetables a Day. Sounds reasonable—until you factor in the rest of the Thou Shalts, as recommended by the school of Fighting Cancer with Food.

Thou Shalt Drink three to four litres of water.

That's anywhere from twelve to sixteen large glasses of water a day. I'm out of bed for about fifteen hours a day, so that means one glass per hour. Allow time for frequent urination; also the aforementioned indelicacy, the thrice-daily measuring of pH levels.

Thou Shalt Drink two glasses of freshly juiced fruit or vegetable juice.

After I've washed an armload of produce and cut it to size for the feed tube, I press it into the machine with so much force I break into sweat. It takes my Fortune 500 juicer about five minutes to grind through all the raw beets and organic kale and carrots I'm stuffing into it. One does not obtain sublime vegetable sap without exercising one's patience.

Before I can guzzle the murky foam, the machinery must be cleaned. Raw beet pulp doesn't get any less stuck to weirdly-shaped juicer organs with the passage of time, so I dismantle the aardvark immediately, turning over each part under running water, scraping inside nooks and crannies with a specially bristled skewer. Through a miracle of vegetable science that I do not quite understand, the magnets in the juice receptacle will keep it nutrient-fresh until I am ready to drink it.

By the time I have drunk the first of my two requisite glasses for the day, at least twenty minutes have passed.

Thou Shalt Drink four ounces of wheatgrass, ideally freshly squeezed.

Wheatgrass is a rich source of folic acid, vitamin B12, and other cancer fighting nutrients. Raw wheatgrass looks like clippings from an abandoned lawn in springtime. Juicing wheatgrass, I discovered, is not unlike loading a ponytail into a drinking straw. Drinking it is worse; it tastes like sweetened paint.

Thou Shalt Consume 70 to 80 percent of your food raw. Chopping and shredding and slicing and grating for approximately twenty minutes will yield enough raw food to satiate my appetite at any given meal. "Good digestion begins in the mouth," Robert O. Young reminds us, "as the saliva produces digestive enzymes that are critical to healthy detoxification and elimination, which in turn are crucial in the fight against cancer."

Chewing said sliced, grated, and shredded raw food takes another twenty minutes. It would not be overstating to say that I spent most of every day attending to some aspect of the cancer-fighting food rules. But here's where it gets tricky: *Thou Shalt Not Drink liquids with meals.*

Apparently fluids drunk too close to eating decelerate the body's natural production of digestive enzymes in the gut. All right, I'll buy that. But how exactly am I supposed to imbibe all those alkalizing liquids, and pop all those mealtime supplements, without drinking liquids with meals?

And where, may I ask, is a gal supposed to find time to, oh I don't know, work? Read? Exercise? Or participate in any other activity that would require leaving the kitchen?

The sheer math of the Gregorian calendar does not allow the meeting of every demand stipulated by the nutritional health zealots.

I feel like a camp counsellor canoeing in the wilderness with twenty-seven children; I can hardly take in the scenery or even paddle the canoe forward, I am so consumed with taking head counts and checking to see that everyone is still above water. My diet has become a circus act. I am a street performer who eats fire while juggling tennis racquets, perched atop a skateboard balancing on a stack of milk cartons. And there are highly risky implications if I don't get all the details just right.

———

I WAS IN MY LAST year of university when I first learned how to make oatmeal chocolate chip cookies. Weirdly, considering more significant life events of which I have no memory, I recall this day in great detail: my friend Sheila's apartment in Montreal's student ghetto, her well-worn burgundy couch, the morning sun puncturing the leaves outside the east-facing window. I was keen to bake some cookies; exams were imminent, stalling and eating were my default study habits. Sheila produced a recipe she had been given by her grandmother, Oatmeal Prune Cookies. Being of healthy twenty-something bowels, we scrapped the prunes in favour of chocolate chips, and a new favourite was born.

The title on my well-worn index card still reads "Sheila's Grandmother's Prune Cookies," a recipe I have followed literally hundreds of times in the intervening years. I have experimented to make it my own, substituting different kinds of chocolate chips, whole grain spelt for wheat flour, quinoa flakes instead of oatmeal. One of the most memorable batches transpired when I impulsively began to bake before assembling all my ingredients—I had the batter half-mixed when I realized I was out of eggs. A quick Google search, conducted through muttered expletives, revealed a brilliant substitute. For the vegans, ovo-allergic, and absent-minded bakers among us, it turns out a bit of ground flax meal mixed with water doubles as an egg (in baking only, not recommended for the morning poach or scramble). The batch was possibly my favourite ever.

Everyone has a romantic weakness; this one is mine. I have a long-standing, tortured, stormy love affair with the oatmeal-prune-without-the-prunes cookie, pulled off the rack when it is still warm, or savoured with a cup of peppermint tea. Every mouthful nourishes me with solace, history, and cheer—and subsequently rockets me into instant and intense self-flagellation over my weak will. I used to kick myself for succumbing to the lover's warm kiss because of its lingering after-effects on my waistline. But now the stakes are significantly higher than a muffin top hanging over skinny jeans. Because I now know—thank you Nancy, thank you Robert O. Young—that sugar nourishes the anima of the cancer cell too. Like converted souls fuelling the powers of Mephistopheles, converted sugars are the elixir of cancer growth.

My skin turns cold every time I think about it; I am queasy with guilt and self-flagellation, tallying all the acid-forming sugary delectables I have gobbled up over the last forty-odd years. Every cookie, every drizzle of maple syrup,

every slice of birthday cake—and yes, every margarita—
has been a dance with death. Did my sweet tooth give me
cancer? How could such a tender lover be so cruel? I resolve
to end the relationship.

lopsided

FROM WHERE DO WE draw strength to enter the room in which part of our body will be cut off?

Four dizzying, researching, vegetable-juicing weeks after diagnosis, today I will undergo surgery. Given the location and size of the tumour, the lumpectomy option—also known as "breast conserving" surgery—was ruled out. Lateral mastectomy, left side; clinical language simplifies, distills a web of physical and emotional impacts into a single act. I will have my left breast removed. I try to remain matter of fact, keep it as simple as that. I walk through the entrance to the hospital, carrying a toothbrush, a change of clothes, a camera, and my son's cozy flannel dinosaur pillow. The pre-op nurse had suggested bringing a pillow to make the car ride home more comfortable, preferably one that was easy to recognize so it wouldn't get mistaken for hospital property. Check.

I am strangely calm, though I admit to a grip in my gut. Stepping over a line I can never recross. I want this cancer out. But what will I look like when it's gone?

I am concentrating hard on being composed, on staying present in the moment. *Psychological resilience*, please help me now. All we have is this moment; that is my cancer mantra. If ever there were a situation that needs improvement, surely this is it. And yet I can do, master, solve or control nothing. I am simply a passenger, observing details, gathering tufts of cheer. There is the softness of my husband's cheek, as I lean my face into his, the familiar comfort of his touch in the pre-op waiting room. There are the colourful birthday cards and posters plastered across the walls of the nursing station.

There is Julie, the porter with the awesome smile—I am bolstered by her distracting banter as she guides us through the maze of identical beige hallways into the Nuclear Medicine Unit, where I am to lie sandwiched inside a machine that resembles a photocopier the size of a Volkswagen. The Nuclear Meds technician there injects my breast with a needle full of radioactive fluid, quite possibly the most horrible sensation I have ever felt—I would rather have my toes sawed off with a comb than experience that injection again. I'm having trouble finding any beauty in this moment.

The Metropolis-style photocopier is a camera that tracks where the radioactive fluid pools in my lymph tissue; the spot where it ends up is the gateway to my lymph nodes, the section the surgeon needs to remove to see if the cancer has spread outside the breast. This is my biggest fear: discovering evidence that the breast was just the beginning, and that the cancer has moved on to open another branch location. The technician notes the spot on the screen and pulls out a Sharpie marker to make an X in the corresponding location on the side of my breast. This massive machine, a highly invasive medical procedure, guided by a low-tech marker;

X marks the spot, the buried treasure. The whimsy of this thought keeps my mind from running ahead to the fear of what comes next.

Julie the porter guides me to the anteroom of the OR. The clock on the wall indicates my surgery time is scheduled to begin in three minutes. As she starts to help me out of my robe Julie notices the colourful box I have been clutching in my left hand and asks, with genuine friendliness, what it contains. I slide open the small latch and lift the green and blue patterned lid to reveal the random assortment of talismans given to me by friends: handwritten messages, carved stones, a dried flower. I tell her how much I need the strength of my loved ones right now, but Julie shakes her head apologetically. "It will have to stay out here," she says. "You can't bring anything into surgery with you." Then, glancing up at the clock as if it may offer permission to bend hospital protocol, she says, in a slightly lowered voice, "Why don't you bring just one of those things ... something you can tuck into the palm of your hand." She winks conspiratorially.

The night before, a package had arrived from Grant's sister, Martha, who lives in South Africa. Inside was a bolstering message of encouragement and a small chunk of rose-coloured rock. The rock was pink quartz, from the Magaliesberg mountains in South Africa, one of the oldest mountain ranges in the world. Martha's note said to keep it close to my body for strength.

And so, clutching a small piece of an ancient mountain in my left hand, I am wheeled into the operating room by three friendly doctors, one of whom is an anesthesiologist named Rob. He whispers to me that if I can think happy thoughts as the anesthesia is going in, I will have happy dreams during the surgery.

I know immediately what to think about.

The previous weekend, Debbie and two other best girl-friends had taken me to the countryside for a pre-mastec-tomy escape. One afternoon, while they were busy getting massages and napping, I decided to venture out alone for a bike ride. At the top of a dauntingly long, steep hill, I paused to consider my options. I had never been in this neck of the woods before; no one knew where I was; my cellphone was on the bedside table back at the guest house. The safest bet was to retrace my steps to get home—which would mean cycling back *up* this massive hill. My first instinct was to turn around and look for another route, but something held me to that spot. I decided to see the downhill as a symbol of what lay ahead, a descent into something I was afraid of, that I would have to climb back out of. So I pushed off, took a gulp of peaceful country air, and careened down the hill.

The joy of coasting downhill is made all the sweeter by its brevity, knowing that even the longest descent will end in some hard work. Resistance slowly returned to my pedal stroke, and I began to note the details of my surroundings, laying out the mental breadcrumbs for the return home. Still thinking about returning to what I had left behind, going back the same way I had come. Perhaps as a consola-tion for the long climb in store, I suddenly felt certain that there was a reason I had come down that big hill, a payoff for taking that risky plunge. For a few moments I pedalled past the halcyon scenery of fields and farmhouses. And then I saw them.

My mind snaps back to a woodsy path far from this road.

"It is the most special flower in Canada," my mother would say, "and it only blooms for a very short time." I remember the rare thrill of seeing a trillium in bloom, never more than one at a time. Here, though, as I rounded the corner, I saw a huge swath of them in a small wooded space by the side of the road. There must have been three hundred trilliums all in one spot, waiting for me. I could hardly breathe.

Tears welled in my eyes. I stood there for a long time, staring at a patch of trilliums and soaking in the beauty of the world. *Everything will be okay*, they seemed to say. Regardless of the outcome.

That's what I thought about as I went under for my surgery. The doctors told me later I had a smile on my face during the operation, not something they see very often.

———

WHEN I THINK ABOUT my husband's hands, my heart reaches up and grabs hold of my throat. Strong fingernails, solid palms, prominent tendons from years of stickhandling. Tennis calluses, writer's finger muscles. When he is having trouble falling asleep, I stroke my fingers across his palm, a caress of comfort. The gentlest touch contains the most love.

What if those trilliums were just trilliums? Not a sign at all. Is the peace we take from nature enough on its own, or does it have to be an indication of future wellness? I want so much for it to be both.

Who will help my husband fall asleep if I am gone?

stripped

I HAVE BEEN STRIPPED of a part of who I was. The round, soft mass of mammary glands and lactation ducts, one half of the performance team that seduced my husband and nursed the children I subsequently bore him, has been removed. In its place is a six-inch scar, a mauve ribbon of healing tissue that weaves from my armpit across my ribs to my sternum like a country road. I sometimes think about what it would be like to drive the gravel road equivalent of that scar: a wild ride, complete with unpredictable curves and invigorating undulations. Best taken at moderate speed.

My ribs are like so many moraines, rising and falling in ways I never realized before, back when they were covered with maternal armament. My left breast, in addition to the other services it has performed, was also a protection of sorts, padding over the cage. Without the buffer of that pectoral adipose tissue, I can see those bony protrusions, evidence of my simple, frail humanity. Underneath all the trappings of the modern, would-be stylish, urban dynamo I like to consider myself to be, I am simply a skeleton, held together by entirely fragile flesh.

That breast muffled the sound of my heart. Now it beats as though behind tissue paper; during a scary movie, it could knock a drink out of my hand. Hot tea cascading down my throat strikes newly exposed surface nerve endings. Sometimes I look down at my chest as I drink, certain that I will see the fluid ripple through my skin as it descends. It's that close. The satisfying swallow of ice cream has been compromised, without the cushion of cozy flesh, by a palpable freeze to the heart; what used to be pure, insouciant pleasure is now accompanied by a little suffering.

———

IN ADDITION TO all the breast tissue on my left side, the surgeon removed three of my lymph nodes to test for any spread of the disease; the sentinel nodes, gatekeepers to the lymphatic system. When breast cancer has spread to the lymph nodes it means the cells have been let loose into the rest of the body; the animals have found a hole in the fence and escaped the barnyard. It is impossible to find them all.

I lay in the recovery room after surgery, a groggy zombie slowly rising from the anesthesia swamp. The first thing I saw was a blurred clock, then a nurse's back. I must have made a noise; the surgeon appeared beside me.

"Were they clear?" I asked. What came out was more of a mumbled moan; it took two more tries before I could get my teeth and lips to articulate the question I was so desperate to have answered.

"Yes," he replied matter-of-factly. "Sentinel lymph nodes all clear."

I squeezed his arm and beamed with delight. Cue the hallelujah chorus. Or so I thought.

My overnight stay on the fifteenth floor of the downtown hospital was a semi-anesthetized blur, intercut with choppy glimpses of the city skyline, lit skyscrapers blinking evidence of functional life beyond this fragile state. Grant stayed by my side as I slipped in and out of wakefulness. He slept in a metal-armed chair, likely the least of his concerns on what must have felt like a very long night. At home, my children slept under hockey-print duvet covers, their soft floppy hair settled onto natural buckwheat pillows. We didn't want them to be alarmed by seeing me so compromised, so they did not visit. They knew their mother would return the next day, different but the same.

Shortly after I awoke, Jake and Sara came to see me, arriving with cheer and love. In my memory they emerge smiling in the middle of a blurred image, like the viewfinder's crispness at the centre of a zoom lens. If they felt any discomfort being back in a hospital setting after the harrowing delivery of their stillborn child only months before, they didn't show it. Together with Grant we celebrated with relief the post-surgery news that my cancer had been localized, contained in the breast alone, and now entirely removed from my body. It was so satisfying, lying butchered on a clean white sheet, to believe that the hardship was singular, and complete; that adjusting to a new physique was the extent of cancer's challenge to my plans.

dancing with loretta

I T WAS SEVERAL DAYS post-surgery before I could actually look at my scar. Debbie bravely took a photograph for me, so I could know, eventually, when I was ready, how grisly it had looked at the beginning. (Months later I summoned the courage to look at the photograph, a close-up of what appears, at first glance, to be Jaws, the metal-mouthed villain from James Bond movies: twenty-four metal staples skittered across a jagged incision, a meandering ruby-red slice, slightly curved in a wan smile. Fanning out from each staple are feather-like wrinkles of skin, the pulls of confused flesh being tugged in an unfamiliar direction, a girdle for my ribs.)

Two days after surgery, I was visited by a short, stocky homecare nurse named Marita. Her strong arms removed my bandages with matronly efficiency. I winced as she yanked the tape, held my breath as she lifted the gauze bandage, which had been sufficiently hefty as to vaguely replicate a breast-like bulge under my shirt. "Looking good!" she exclaimed, somewhat robotically. My eyes roamed the room, desperate to focus on anything but the devastation Marita was admiring on my front. She bent down, out of my line of vision, muttering and clucking as she rifled through her kit bag. "I left my large bandages in the car, I'll be back in a couple of minutes," she said, brushing past me toward the door. I sat topless on my bed, examining every inch of my ceiling, a prude being taunted with dirty pictures, determined not to look. My gaze landed out the window. The trees, must keep my eyes on the trees. My shape felt altered; it related differently with the space around it. Young blossoms, pink and white, swelling with growth; must not look down. The spring air in my room touched fresh flesh. I could feel the gaping absence, though my eyes saw only bloom. On her daily post-op visits, slightly winded from climbing all the stairs from the street to my bedroom, Marita nonetheless managed to advise me on how to make sense of what had happened to me. "I became a Christian after I had uterine cancer in 2007," she reminded me most days. "I had been eating well, living my life right, but I still got cancer. I realized, lying there recovering the way you are now, that I hadn't read the Bible enough and that's why I got sick." She went on to assure me that I shouldn't worry, what had happened to me was not unique. "I take out drainage tubes and remove staples every single day, all over the city. What has happened to you happens to women all the time, every day." As though that was a good thing, normalizing the disfigurement of a young woman's body. I didn't bother asking her if she thought more women were getting cancer because of the toxins in our environment, because of the chemicals in the products we put on our skin every day, because lax government standards and shoddy regulations for chemical testing mean we are all walking science experiments. I didn't have the energy for any moralizing. There simply wasn't room in my heart for the requisite anger.

The Sunday following my surgery was Mother's Day. I know my family gathered at our house to celebrate, but I have only the foggiest memory of the occasion, my first time out of pyjamas in nearly a week. There were flowers, delicious food made by my mother, and the warmth of family closeness. Hugs were executed gingerly. I was too groggy and sore to think then about what a hard day that must have been for Jake and Sara to celebrate. Mother's Day was a day my brother and I both spent in pain.

After a couple of weeks, my scar healed enough for me to put something other than a folded sock into my bra cup, so my mother took me breast shopping. The post-op nurses had sent me home with a list of breast retailers (I love to imagine the ad campaign for such establishments: *"Breasts, boobs, titties! Get your jugs right here, ladies—left, right, or both! Big ones, small ones, we got 'em all. They won't sag 'cuz they're made o' rubber. Get yourself a new set of cans today!"*). We made our way to the nearest one. Actually, it was a lingerie and swimwear shop that also sold breasts (though no other body parts). Well-heeled customers with both boobs intact perused the racks of silks and satins right alongside me—and my sports-sock substitute. My mother approached a full-figured saleswoman in a navy sweater with glasses on a chain around her neck, and they began to speak in hushed tones. I wandered further down the room, feeling conspicuous. Shiny white mannequins with perfect—balanced—figures bookended every rack in the store, wearing shimmery turquoise bras, glamorous mauve teddies, lacy pink panties. Each struck a casual yet imperious pose, conjuring more sex appeal with their stiff plastic bodies than I could imagine ever feeling again with my real flesh. Their white eyes stared at me blankly. The saleswoman smiled kindly as she approached, and asked how I was feeling. As I replied, she pursed her lips and tilted her head as if to size me up, then retreated to the back of the store. A moment later, the saleswoman returned with a box marked *4 L*, and ushered me into a private changing room. My mother waited outside on a cushioned bench. I wondered if she was thinking about the time we went bra shopping for my first 32A (*"Let it be Dici or nothing"*) as she watched her single-breasted daughter disappear behind the door.

The change room had the air of a starlet's backstage quarters; an enormous mirror took up most of one wall, camisoles and robes hung on hooks along another. A sepia-toned photograph in an antique frame showed a woman in a lacy cotton slip casually bent over to undo a garter, a strap having slipped off her shoulder, revealing a small white breast. Innocently sexual, she seemed unaware of being photographed. Would I ever feel that unselfconscious about my misshapen form? While she fiddled with the plastic wrap on the box, the saleswoman asked me to remove my top. Her tone was gentle, casual, without any concern for the sundered frontage I was about to reveal. I began to undo my buttons, turning away from the saleswoman to discreetly remove the sports sock. I leaned over a side table covered with a series of shiny blue packages marked "Disposable Hypoallergenic Thong," and dropped the sock into my purse. Just then the saleswoman's struggle with the package wrapper subsided. "There we go! At last," she said. I turned to see her open the box to reveal a flesh-coloured lump resting in a cradle of white moulded plastic. Lifting the breast as though it were a museum treasure, some kind of rare antique Jell-O, she tenderly placed it in the empty cave of my bra cup. "Wow, you're good," I commented, when her first guess proved to be the right size. The saleslady lowered her glasses to dangle across her sizable frontage, looked me in the eye and gave me a rueful, closed-lipped smile. "My dear," she said softly, "I do this every day."

And with that, the bond with my plastic pal began. I considered calling it Loretta, but the relationship is more practical than affectionate; it lives inside my bra and gets hoisted into place every morning without fanfare. Occasionally I think of the daily shimmy into my bra as dancing with Loretta; the shift into position, the tug toward the sternum. C'mon, Loretta, let's face a new day together. There's something cartoonish about a prosthetic breast. My friend Honor remembers visiting her grandmother and playing with her prostheses. She would arrive at the house wearing her Brownie uniform with two little flap pockets on the front of her shirt, knowing her grandmother would let her put the falsies in the pockets to pretend she had breasts. That's about as sexy as I feel with Loretta: like I'm wearing a Brownie uniform at my grandmother's house. Blessedly, I have a husband who loves me for my smile more than my symmetry. Though its powers to seduce an adult are limited, the fascination of the falsie where a child is concerned cannot be denied. One day I came into my room after a shower and found nine-year-old Harper coddling my 4 L. His lean-fingered hand caressed the curvaceous pink lump, his cinnamon-brown eyes wide with delight and intrigue. He looked like a student in a pre-teen groping lesson, practising the art of the fondle on a plastic dummy. It's hard to take a rubber breast seriously. When I take it off at the end of the day, I often touch the smooth flat surface that rides against my ribs and scar, and marvel at Loretta's warmth. But of course it is actually mine.

splitting and multiplying

ONE ACADEMIC FOOTNOTE stands apart in my memory's hazy blur of secondary school studies, likely due to its spectacular amount of *room for improvement*. I achieved a particularly poor result on a grade nine biology test when I confused the meanings of *mitosis* and *meiosis*. Why two different types of cell division need to have such similar-sounding names is a question many high school science students have likely asked before and since my epic flub. *Meiosis*, I have never forgotten since, refers to the splitting and multiplying of reproductive cells, those found in eggs and sperm. In what could be considered strikingly miraculous conditions—the presence of just the right amount of gonadotropin-releasing hormone, which in turn triggers the production of follicle-stimulating hormone, which in turn stimulates luteinizing hormone, which allows for the creation of testosterone in the male and estrogen in the female—conception takes place. Gametes, or single-sex cells, from each party contain only twenty-three chromosomes; seeking completion, they find a match and together form a diploid cell, containing the full human complement of forty-six chromosomes. With that nifty alignment of order taken care of, pairs of matching chromosomes arranged neatly in their place, *mitosis* can begin: the regular and ongoing division of cells and multiplication of new ones. Mitosis allows an organism to grow from a single cell to trillions of cells. Mitosis, you might say, allows a dream, a shared love, a hope for legacy to grow into a soft-skinned baby boy or girl.

What I did not know in grade nine is that cancer is essentially a disease of mitosis—repeated, uncontrolled mitosis that overtakes the system like a horde of bargain-hungry shoppers. When a healthy cell is damaged (from air pollution? The lye in grandma's soap? Too many oatmeal chocolate chip cookies?), it mutates into a cancer cell. Compared to its normal counterparts, a cancer cell looks dirty, pocked, and unpolished. Its edges are rougher; a microscopic bully. Hopped up on its own might, the cancer cell quickly throws the mitosis lever into high gear. After five days of normal cell division, a healthy single-cell organism will grow to achieve roughly thirty-two cells; in the same time period, a cancerous cluster explodes into one thousand four hundred and eighty cells, the beginnings of a tumour. By the time it has a million cells, the tumour is the size of a BB gun pellet.

At twenty-one days in the building of a human, the zygote has graduated to blastocyst and nestles in for an extended stay in the womb. A week later, it has grown to a double layer of cells, the life force hard at work dividing and multiplying. Neurogenesis begins, the first steps in sparking up brain activity in the tiny developing form. It becomes an embryo, from the Greek for *that which grows.*

Somewhere along this well-worn evolutionary pathway, for infertile couples mitosis simply stops. Perhaps it shuts

down due to insufficient pituitary hormones: too little testosterone in the male partner, oligospermia (too few sperm),
or asthenozoospermia (abundant but sluggish). It could be
caused by invisible complications with a female's encoded
proteins—the follitropin subunit beta or the forkhead box,
whimsical names for devastating genetic mutations. And
sometimes, in cases of healthy weight, non-smoking parents
who are guilty of nothing but taking a little longer to find
each other in the crowd, it is what doctors call idiopathic:
arising spontaneously, from an obscure or unknown cause.

Normal cells have a built-in feature that measures
surrounding cell growth in the area, shutting down when
density is maximized; methodical and shipshape, a human
cell lives by the practical mantra *A place for everything, and
everything in its place*. When just enough cells have been
produced to form an eyelash, production stops. Job well
done.

Cancer cells ignore the density-dependent inhibition of
growth. They continue to pile up, running out the production system until all nutrients are exhausted. Starting at its
most infinitesimal state, cancer creates disarray and imbalance. A catastrophic mess.

In other words, both infertility and cancer are complications of mitosis; in the one it is desperately stalled, in
the other it is a runaway train. Both are cases of untidy,
broken systems, lacking order. On the most basic, microscopic level, that pleasing pattern of precise execution,
properly sequenced steps designed to achieve appropriate
results, went awry for both my brother and me. Our very
cells scorned the checks and balances of Just So operations,
ignoring how it should be. Beyond the reach of control.

the fairy princess

H UGE TREES FILL the view through the floor-to-ceiling windows of the cancer centre where my post-surgical treatment was to continue. Cancer surgeons are just that: cut-and-stitch experts who remove cancer's growth and reassemble what's left of the body afterwards. For the next steps, post-op, my surgeon had referred me to a medical oncologist at a different hospital. As I entered the building with my husband for our first appointment, I was struck by the abundance of light that filtered through the branches outside and lit the two-storey space; architecturally it resembled a modern, downtown mall, only with paltry shopping options. This space would come to be very familiar, even mind-numbingly routine over the ensuing months; on this initial visit, though, it felt like walking into a huge, crowded club I never knew existed. Blue-vested volunteer greeters proffered cookies (feeding sugar to cancer patients!); bald men and women stood in lines, sat slumped in chairs. We walked past them toward the tree-studded windows and sat down to wait. My medical oncologist turned out to be a rosy-cheeked blonde with fabulous taste in shoes. She burst into that and every subsequent appointment with such confidence and optimism, I took to calling her the Fairy Princess. Just seeing her made me hopeful. She talked us through the bewildering minutiae of treatment scenarios. The space inside my ears went numb; I caught words intermittently. Chemotherapy ... extensive metabolizer ... menopause ... estrogen receptors ... My husband took notes; I tried to concentrate but found I couldn't absorb the oncological detail. I wondered where the Fairy Princess had bought her shoes. When we were done, she sent me for blood work down the hall and across the building to the pharmacy to fill the first of many prescriptions.

———

THOUGH IT IS CHOCK-A-BLOCK with countless medicaments for every one of cancer's cruel symptoms and its treatment's side effects, the hospital pharmacy is strangely calm, an oasis of managed exactitude. Outside its doors, the fluid chaos of cancer care is in constant motion. Patients shuffle in and out of treatment; nurses clutching charts dash to intercept a doctor or catch the elevator; caregivers advocate in full voice, their exasperation overriding privacy concerns. The doors at the building's entrance slide open and closed with a metronome's steady beat. The cancer centre is a vibrant hub, busy and alive with those battling death. But inside the pharmacy, there is a prevailing stillness; care has been taken to create the illusion of order. Smooth white shelves are neatly lined with rows of medication, each in a tailored, pleasantly coloured package. Eight packages of Senokot ("gentle overnight relief for occasional constipation") are stacked in symmetrical sequence: two rows, two high, two deep. Biotene toothpaste ("specially formulated not to irritate a dry mouth"): six boxes in a tidy stack. Pink packs of Gravol stand in a straight row, their rosy package flaps fan in precision. Notrimaderm, OroNat, Neutragel, Bisacodyl; meaningless brand names mask medicinal potency. Monistat, Lacteeze, Polytopic, Urigard, Bag Balm; the promise of relief for cancer's litany of physical humiliations is laid out with the welcome harmony of pattern. Pill splitters, pill crushers, pill boxes, super pill boxes, weekly pill planners; each takes their place in a meticulous display. These shelves fill me with terror—what agonies lie ahead? And yet their tidy arrangement holds the promise of control, predictability: cancer made manageable. As though there were any order to this madness. I hesitate before stepping back out the doorway. How could a neon-lit sales centre for overpriced pharmaceuticals feel like a temple? I notice how much comfort I take from the illusion of order.

By the end of our appointment, the Fairy Princess had helped us decide to include me in a clinical trial the hospital was conducting with a lab in California, a precise genomic analysis comparing ten thousand international samples of estrogen receptor–positive invasive lobular carcinoma—my particular form of the disease—to determine how dependent my cancer cells were on estrogen and how they would react to chemotherapy or drug treatments. By identifying more specifics about my pathology, we could determine the best course of treatment for this particular cancer. And so, while my left arm finger-walked up the walls, leaned against door frames to re-establish mobility, and my right arm grated raw beets and sliced collard greens to alkalize my environment, my tumour got on a plane to California. We were told we would have to wait three weeks for the results—which left me some time to take matters into my own hands.

the war on cancer

ONCE SHE'D CONVINCED me to remove any threat of cooked food from my diet, Nancy went on to inform me that the E in her TAPE acronym could be resolved by EFT, in which she was a highly trained practitioner; she could offer me a session right now.

"EFT?" I asked, bracing for whatever might come next in this unusual appointment.

"Emotional Freedom Technique. It's a therapy in which the patient directs positive thought toward their childhood, giving up anxieties that were held as a child."

"But I think I had a pretty happy childhood, I don't really have any extraordinary memories of trauma or sadness that I feel the need to ... uh, free."

"You may have emotional baggage from when you were a toddler. Let me look into your eyes."

I spent the next twenty minutes with Nancy as she looked into each of my irises and said she could see the fissure in my eyeball that represented cancer; it was a small, short crack, so I wasn't to worry too much. Oh how I wanted, right then, for iridology to be a legitimate science. I wanted nothing more than to believe that my future with breast cancer could be measured by blood vessels around my cornea. She then talked me through some Emotional Freedom, trolling my subconscious for painful memories. Anxious that I wasn't really coming up with much cancer-curing emotional fodder, I half-heartedly conjured the best insult I could think of on the spot: being dumped by my first boyfriend, Nick.

As I pulled out my cheque book and handed over a cool $150, I wanted to ask whether Nancy thought the MRI next week would show that the tumour had suddenly begun to evaporate as a result of my accepting that I was still a great person, in spite of Nick once thinking otherwise. But I didn't dare. She had offered to pray for me and to send me some raw food recipes that she thought I might like. She really did mean well.

I left her office feeling a queasy mixture of optimism and shame. Nancy was the first alternative cancer-care practitioner I had ever met or heard of, but she wouldn't be the last. David Servan-Schreiber, MD, a two-time cancer survivor and best-selling author of *Anticancer: A New Way of Life*, approached the disease with a maxim I could relate to: You would be crazy, he wrote, not to use the proven success of Western medicine's tools (surgery, chemotherapy, and radiation) to fight your cancer. But you would be equally crazy to *only* use those tools. What he did not mention is that, in the face of a life-threatening disease, *crazy* becomes a relative term. Diagnosis with any serious illness has the power to draw out alternative health remedies—quacks and healers both. There are a great many cancer patients whose recovery protocols involve multiple treatments in hospital, myriad doctors appointments, a slew of prescription refills, and nothing more. But if you're open to alternative thinking that extends beyond Western oncology—or if you're desperate to get the disharmony of ill health under control— the options are legion. You could have your blood passed through a frequency generator ("electromedicine" that converts cancer cells back into normal cells); guzzle jugfuls of Limu juice (a seaweed-based concoction containing cancer-killing fucoidan); take high doses of vitamin C by intravenous (advocated by two-time Nobel Prize winner Dr. Linus Pauling); boost your intake of laetrile (vitamin B17, banned by the FDA but found naturally in apricot kernels; it is recommended to take between twenty-four and forty kernels a day—proponents recommend planting an apricot tree in your backyard); experiment with the Brandt grape cure (NOT, advocates insist, the Wortman grape cure!); boost your nutritional enzyme count with an exclusively raw diet (Nancy's method of choice); pop Barefoot Calcium (coral calcium pills to be taken with every meal, blended into powder for better absorption); consume hydrogen peroxide (but not in conjunction with the Budwig Diet!); obey the Bob Beck Protocol (drinking ionic colloidal silver in combination with magnetic microcurrent electrotherapy); drink methyl-sulfonomethane water ("Free Ground Shipping to the entire US up to $150!"). Always, the exclamation point.

Since 1971, when Richard Nixon declared "War on Cancer," the number of cancer cases has risen dramatically— especially among people under age fifty; the average person's risk of being diagnosed has gone up, not down—you're 50 percent more likely to get cancer today, Dear Reader, than when America's cancer war began. As comical as this litany of quackery may seem to the healthy reader, the appeal of lateral thinking swells exponentially when one's own health is under siege. Suddenly the medical establishment's inching pace toward victory doesn't seem a sufficient battle plan. To read the analysis at Quackwatch.com, these alternative therapies are charlatans, defrauding the vulnerable at their weakest hour. Still, I wonder. The most confounding alternative remedy I have come across is an herbal formula called Essiac, created in 1922 by a Canadian nurse named René Caisse. Made with plants used in traditional Native healing, Essiac (Caisse spelled backwards) has had a remarkable success rate in healing cancer patients. A stack of Essiac research sits on my desk: a 160-page thesis examines how the mainstream medical establishment botched scientific testing of the formula; *The Essiac Report: Canada's Remarkable Unknown Cancer Remedy* explores why the Western medical establishment doesn't want a simple herbal tea recipe to shut off the flow of private and public funding of the search for a cancer cure; *Essiac: A Native Herbal Cancer Remedy* includes testimonials from patients who went from "death's door" to the pinnacle of health. A Post-it note stuck to the back reminds me this last book came from my mother-in-law. The note reads: "W.B. gave me this for you. She had the same thing as you eighteen years ago and is the picture of health." I have a bottle of Essiac in my pantry—a remedy for cancer! On sale at the health food store up the road from my house! Why hasn't the press been notified? For whatever reason, I cannot conjure the emotional conviction for this option. The bottle of Essiac in my pantry remains unopened. My mother paid a small fortune to buy me a contraption called the BioMat, having been assured of its cancer cell–killing virtues. It is a brown cloth mat about six feet long and three feet wide, stitched with padded ribs and packed tight with amethyst crystals. When the package arrived from Hawaii, it took two postal carriers to lug it onto my porch. Setting it up was like trying to arrange an inebriated lumberjack into a yoga pose. One end of the mat plugs into the wall; a dashboard of flickering red and green LED lights intercepts any negative ions from the electrical charge and converts them to positive ions. We don't want negative ions, no. Apparently the positive ions create heat that radiates through the amethysts to create the far infrared spectrum of light, which is capable of healing tissue, reducing inflammation, and killing cancer cells. I'm not actually sure that makes scientific sense, but I like the sound of it. I consider myself to be at least a moderately capable reader, but the promotional literature that shipped with the mat was such airy, New Age gobbledygook, I truly couldn't understand what it said. But I can tell you that my new nickname for the mat is the Mind Eraser, so blissful is the trance it quickly induces. Resting on it makes my body intensely warm, and yet the mat itself is not hot to the touch. If I crank up the dials on the dashboard it can make me sweat like a Swedish sauna. I have no idea whether it is in fact killing any rogue cancer cells, but I lie down on that crazy deadweight slab every chance I get. When certainty is not available, isn't hope on a warm mat a worthwhile pursuit? I'm still looking for the right way out of this mess. Kierkegaard said, "Faith begins precisely where thinking leaves off." In other words, we do not decide to have faith, it is a purely emotive response to a situation; it cannot withstand the scrutiny of reason. Which must mean that the attempt to summon faith is futile; it either exists in the gut or it doesn't.

wired for accomplishment

SOMETIMES I PLAY Cancer Centre Waiting Room Math. Puzzle tables: 3. Back issues of *CAA Magazine, Retirement Living*, and *Zoomer*: 7. White-haired women with bearded, balding husbands: 11. Overweight men in ball caps: 8 (with canes: 3). Fifty-plus bald, eyebrowless women with headscarves, knitting: 6. Obese women wearing tight tank tops and orthotics: 4. Rosy-cheeked vegetarians with children in primary school and organic cotton tampons in their purse: 1.

Why the fuck did I get cancer? It's not all that fun a game; I always wind up frustrated. Why indeed? Some people think there is a biological reason for getting cancer—genetic mutation, estrogen overload, exposure to toxins—and also a spiritual reason. "Cancer is a message," someone once told me. "If you don't hear the message the first time, it comes back again. Louder." What admonition rode on the back of that diagnosis? If cancer is a caution light on the dashboard, forcing me onto the gravel shoulder, what does it have to say about the road I have travelled? And isn't attributing cancer to some attitude or behaviour I did or did not possess some version of blaming the victim?

Yet the idea of cancer's message is one I cannot shake. What is it about my life that I might need to change?

Most people who get cancer decide to start eating less meat, buy organic vegetables, clean their homes with fewer chemicals. Sheryl Crow hung up her cellphone; Suzanne Somers took up yoga; Lance Armstrong stopped being an asshole. (Or so we thought for a while.)

Those cancer epiphany options are not available in this case. So what is cancer trying to tell me?

———

BY THIS POINT, a few weeks after my surgery, I was feeling like a bit of a superstar: cancer was a test, and I had scored an A. My mastectomy was successful (sounds like an oxymoron, I know); I had fought hard to see the top surgical oncologist who had left me with what all the nurses said was his signature scar, perfectly executed. (Good, I liked having a perfect scar.) My drainage tubes came out two days earlier than average, a medical pat on the head for good behaviour. Marita the nurse said my healing was coming along beautifully (she may even have used the word *perfectly*). Head down, best foot forward, I got through it. I even remembered to document the journey with photographs and journal entries. I was acing cancer—incorporating its inconvenience into my plans and continuing along my way. I couldn't possibly have known that all my conviction was misplaced.

Witty, upbeat email missives to friends and family? Check. Strict cancer-fighting food regimen? Check. Regular physio exercises to regain mobility? Check. Alternative healing protocols? Sure, why not. Bonus check. Wired for accomplishment, I had nailed the beast and hung its head on my front door. Friends and family never felt closer. I added their goodness to my list of inoculations.

surrounded

*D*o YOU HAVE *a cooler you can put on your porch for meal delivery?*

Meals are coming starting Monday ... Look for a dramatic rise in hits to vegan blogs.

What are your child care needs? Is someone on this? I have lots of willing hands offering to help and eventually will run out of jobs for them so might be able to pass off child care. Do you need me to be your nanny?

Where do you take your dry cleaning? What else needs doing? (Please don't get a dog yet!)
Lisa

I am great at all "who the hell wants to think about cancer today?" avoidance strategies. Please call me for manicures, spa days, long walks, dancing, bookstore visits, or pure optimism sessions.
Sarah

I haven't prayed since I was twelve, but I'm going to now.
Love, David

I am on board for screaming obscenities at the moon. I'll
come by tonight.
Grazyna

Call me anytime, day or night, & I'll be there in the fastest
four-hour drive—cooking, cleaning your toilets, digging out
your front garden, and playing with your hair.
Love, Sheila

You may feel scared and kind of alone—but you're not.
We got you surrounded sister and we're all going to help you
get through this. I promise.
Love, Mike

———

WHILE WE WAITED for California test results, I juiced, chopped raw vegetables, and practised my arm rehab exercises three times every day to help regain mobility on my left side. And I checked email with Christmas-morning enthusiasm. Every day, without fail, I received loving, emboldening messages from friends and family, the kind that make you feel certain that everything will be all right.

One day I had a visit from a friend who was going through the awkward contortions of a complicated divorce. She was thin, exhausted, and spent. We laughed and cried over our respective crises, each more concerned about the other's plight than our own. Sitting on my couch, her pale hands cupping a mug of tea, she described a visualization exercise recommended by her therapist as a coping strategy when the anguish of disassembling her family felt like too much.

"She had me close my eyes, sitting there in her office, and envision all the people that I know and love in the world, and all the people who love me. Then she told me to picture them holding hands or linking arms and forming a circle around me. So now sometimes I close my eyes and do it on my own. I find it's a really helpful exercise to think about when I am feeling down, imagining that ring of love and care encircling me, picturing all the people out there to prop me up and keep me safe."

Listening intently to her explanation, I felt as though I had been kicked in the head with a warm golden boot, such was the shock of realizing something so uplifting all at once. I was intimately acquainted with that feeling of being surrounded by people who loved me, but I realized that now I didn't have to close my eyes to see them. The set of locked arms encircling me was woven through the streets of my neighbourhood. The circle bulged out and widened to include friends and supporters from across town and across the map. Every bit of fear and suffering I felt was buttressed, ounce for ounce, by the nurturing strength around me. The nature of love and friendship is a one-two punch: the act or gesture that demonstrates it is the first gift—the meal, the ride, the phone call—but the very fact of the gesture is the second—the existence of that caring sentiment in the first place. The knowledge that we are loved lasts even longer than the loving itself. For me it has become an inflatable chariot that carries me through the dark and craggy tunnel of cancer, buffering the rough edges and softening the blows around sharp turns.

The loving acts themselves take many forms. The first was probably the spreadsheet created by my friend Lisa to coordinate cooking help (Grant's energies already spread thin these days as primary caregiver and sole breadwinner). She marshalled volunteers into a scheduled service that operated with military precision. Meals were made and delivered four nights a week, accommodating each of the curious dietary challenges presented by various members of my family. High alkaline vegan meals for the nutrition-obsessed cancer patient, legume-free for the peanut-, garbanzo-, and lentil-allergic son, plus a little naturally raised organic meat for the weary environmentalist husband, bearing the caregiver's physical and psychological load. Night after night, no two meals were ever the same; no one missed their delivery. At five-thirty we would check the cooler on the front porch like children opening a birthday gift, wide-eyed with anticipation and the gurgly, effervescent sensation of warmth below the sternum when someone makes you feel special. Meal after meal my family and I ate like kings, invisible staff having lightened our burden. Food made with love lands in the belly with the accompaniment of distant music.

I had been on the giving end of the meal brigade before. It is a universal tool for community care—because the process of nurturing someone in your circle is mutually beneficial. Those providing random acts of kindness feel empowered, as a relief from helplessness but also as an assertion of personal survival. The act of signing up for a tour of meal-delivery duty is somehow a form of resistance to bad news for oneself. I am well, I am able; I will do what I can because I can. As much as it is a deeply heartfelt gesture of support and caring for the wounded bird in the flock, it is also a reaffirmation of the health and well-being of the helper.

Errands were run for us. I would leave some cash and a list of random household needs (toothbrush, light bulbs, white vinegar) in the mailbox; by the end of the day the requested items were on the porch. One evening we answered the door to find my son Reggie's hockey coach—a neighbour whom we had always been fond of but could not claim to know well—carrying an enormous empty hockey bag, offering to fill it with our dirty laundry and return it the next day, cleaned and folded. On a sunny spring morning just days after my surgery I came downstairs to find my mother, Sara, my friend Grazyna, and her mother standing in my backyard, outfitted in work clothes and gardening gloves. They had committed their precious Saturday to do all my spring planting, transforming my gritty grey post-winter yard into a colourful delight, sowing hope and the promise of growth with every turn of the trowel.

I sat on a garden chair and watched them work—an effete doer, sidelined. I watched Grazyna's mother tuck stray wisps of hair deftly into her bun as she hunched over my flowerbeds, my sister-in-law wiping her forehead with the base of her dirty glove. The humble acceptance of weakness was a revelation to me. Letting others love you is itself an act of love.

———

JAKE TOOK MY BOYS for weekend sleepovers, ferried them to hockey games, and cheered them on at their school play in their parents' absence. We joked that he was so well-trained in handling kids, he'd be overqualified when he finally had one of his own. We didn't talk about how unlikely that was ever to come to pass, we just kept up the ruse that it would. Jake and Sara kept their grieving to themselves all those months of my treatment; it mustn't have ever stopped hurting, but they became master illusionists themselves.

Miles had turned six just before my surgery. Try as I might, I couldn't pull together anything resembling a celebration. So I took a few friends up on those if-you-ever-need-anything-just-call offers. I said I was worried about Miles interpreting the lack of a sixth birthday party as further evidence that his world was turning upside down after cancer struck our family. As it turns out, people really mean it when they say they'll help with whatever you might need. The greater challenge is to believe we deserve the rescue. Women are so adept at taking the role of caretaker and provider of strength, we can easily forget how to be vulnerable and in need; we are trained to do more, do it perfectly, and not admit to the strain. No magazines instruct us on How to Be Okay with Being Beggared, How to Ask for Help When You're Strapped, How to Do Less. At first I was racked with guilt at the gathering of willing hands ready to make a meal, never mind throw a birthday party. *They have four children to look after, how can they be feeding my big family on top of it all? She has a huge job; the idea of caring for me must be causing her so much stress. I must be such a burden ...* But I had no choice. I simply did not have the strength or focus (or time, frankly, cancer being the full-time job that it is) to look after everything myself. Cancer forced me from my position of strength, dethroned the overachieving Uber-Mom who can Do It All.

Miles blew out his six candles on a homemade Pokémon birthday cake that would have made Martha Stewart proud, delivered with a smile by my friend Cathy. Debbie and Lisa threw him a birthday party a couple of weeks later. I sat on the sidelines of the festivities, weak and sore, yet swollen with blessings. How could I be feeling so fortunate when I had just undergone a disfiguring major surgery for a life-threatening disease?

I found a study in the *Journal of Experimental Social Psychology* in which researchers asked individuals to stand at the base of a steep hill with a heavy pack on their backs and estimate how challenging it would be to get to the top. The participants standing with a friend consistently gauged the ascent to be less steep and the pack to be less heavy, compared with those who were standing alone; the longer the study participants had known their friends, the gentler they estimated the incline to be. Technically, having been a cancer patient for several weeks now, I have never been in poorer health. Yet I cannot remember ever feeling so well, or so blessed—sharing the load and finding pleasure in the uphill climb.

the g word

THE ROOM IN THE Quaker meeting house is large, filled with rows of church-basement chairs: metal legs, curved plastic seats, easily stackable. The rows form several semicircles, cascading out from a small table in the centre of the room. On top of the table is an ordinary-looking vase containing a single bloom: a pale pink camellia slightly past its peak, more backyard flowerbed than high-priced florist. Beyond the flower, seen through a large picture window that takes up most of the north wall of the room, is a garden. The view is rich with spring's growth, though the colour palette is limited; green grass, darker green shrubbery with a few yellow blossoms, flowerbeds that appear to be untended of late, with only a few pale pink flowers dotting the overgrowth, and several tall pines towering over the scene.

My friend Andy has brought me here to a Sunday morning service, a favourite experience he wants to share with me as I prepare to go through my treatment. We look for seats, midway back, sidling along the row until we are just past halfway around the curve. We sit. Andy has attended a Quaker service before and has prepared me for the simplicity of the process. There is no liturgy, no leader,

no sermon, no readings. So I sit. And I wait, though I can't
say for what.

I look out the window. I try to appreciate the stillness,
the silence in this cavernous room. I peek surreptitiously at
the other half dozen people sprinkled throughout the space.
Are they all Quakers? Is this their weekly ritual or have they
stumbled in here as I have, looking for some solace during
a particular period of madness? I try to spot any uncomfortable shifting and covert peering around, the sure sign
of an interloper such as myself. But they all appear to be
more practised at this meditative communing. I stare out
the window some more. I concentrate on taking pleasure
from the simple, natural beauty of the plants in the garden.
A squirrel scales one of the pine trees, a bird lands on
a branch; I try to attach weight to this simple sighting of
urban wildlife, try to achieve some kind of peace from the
timelessness of the natural world. I scratch my left ankle. I
roll my head around on my neck and listen to the crackles.
I rub behind my ear. I'm feeling restless, bored, anxious for
someone to say something. Do I have anything to say? I
rack my brain for any insights, but find no wisdom worthy
of breaking this silence. I close my eyes. Now at least I look
the part: ponderous sophisticate contemplating meaningful
thoughts in her own private reverie. But when I close my
eyes I begin to think about cancer, about the discomfort on
my left side, the numbness around my scar. I start to worry
about how much sicker I will feel as my treatment continues,
how much it will hurt, how hard it will be on my kids to
see me go through it. I recognize the beginning steps of the
dance of anxiety, the panic around whether or not I will die
from this cancer, the slow rumble of fear that can build to a

whirling dervish of despair, careening through my mind like a drunk with a dripping paintbrush, smearing unease and doubt all over the walls of my composure.

I open my eyes. Not gonna go there. I have come to visualize those moments as the switch point on a train track; there's a lever that an engineer can pull to slide the track over from one set of rails to another, rerouting the train. That train of gloom can build up such speed, so quickly, and it only ever ends in a gory crash that serves no benefit to anyone. So I realign the rails for a steadier ride, opening my eyes to what is right in front of me; away from fear of the future and straight into the simplicity of the present.

The garden is no more colourful or better groomed when I open my eyes, but its comforts are significantly magnified somehow by the shift in my thinking. I watch the wind gracefully swaying the branches of the trees, always a salve for my spirits. A calm eases through me, like slow warmth from a heating pad. I still don't know what I'm supposed to think about or feel for the next fifty minutes of this service, but for the moment I have found a shred of peaceful succour.

I am continuing my attempts to zone in on this kind of equable interpretation of the simple flower alone in the vase on the table, when a voice somewhere to my right begins to speak. Showtime at last!

Turning my head I see a man with sandy brown hair and beard, possibly my age, early forties. He wears off-white linen shorts and a pale shirt patterned with thin stripes; both are rumpled, the shirt is untucked. He is talking to the centre of the room, as if addressing the flower more than any of the rest of us seated in his company.

"I went through a very difficult time a couple of years

ago, a terribly challenging period in my life," he says, then pauses.

I comb his appearance for clues to determine what he might have gone through: is he scrawny and pale, recovering from a terrible illness? Is he gay? Did he lose a lover? Is there a wedding band, or could he be referring to the bitter ending of a relationship?

He continues to speak, shifting his gaze between the middle of the room and the floor in front of him. "What I learned going through that experience is that the more I find in my life to be grateful for, the more God gives me to be grateful for."

The G word kind of throws me. For a moment I fail to really digest all of what he has said, hung up on that one word, trying to interpret why he used it. Was he an interloper too? Perhaps he had strayed from the strictness of a particular set of dogma in search of a more relaxing approach to spirituality, but brought the language of his old church along with him? I had thought of Quakers as being more secular than that, more interested in social justice than religious doctrine, keen to serve humanity more than any divine power. But perhaps I was wrong. The room is silent again, bearded man back in his chair. No one is reacting to his comment, at least not out loud.

Hmm, a fairly short show, I thought. I half-hoped for more speakers to rise and air their thoughts, though a part of me did want to get back to that serene contemplation of the garden.

It wasn't until long after the meeting ended that Sunday morning, after Andy and I had shaken hands with everyone on the way out of the room, politely declined their offers of coffee and biscuits, and wandered back into the imperfect bustle and hubbub of the city, that I began to really consider what the bearded man had said. In the end, he wasn't the only one to speak during the meeting. Two other people had also broken the silence over the course of the hour: one recommending a spiritual film he had been particularly moved by recently, the other ruminating on violence and the human spirit after having witnessed a street fight during his night shift at a downtown hostel. There were no discussions, no dialogue, no follow up to any of the points made.

But in my mind tonight, the dialogue continues. I'm not sure how to make sense of spirituality, especially in light of the illness I was struck with. I envy people who can put complete faith in a god or a heaven or some other imperturbable interpretation that makes sense of our complicated world, but I can't go there myself.

The idea of gratitude, though, is more palatable to me; an emotional and spiritual landscape that I am starting to travel with more ease. I figure I can be grateful for things without having to be grateful to any one spirit or provider.

And so I begin, taking my cue from this stranger in the rumpled linen shorts. I lie in bed and begin to consider the events, the people, the images and things around me for which I am grateful. Andy's kindness in sharing the Quaker service with me, the tangy-sweet burst of raspberries in this morning's breakfast bowl, the soft pale skin of my husband's arm lying beside me.

Making a nightly tally of gratitudes contained within each day becomes a soothing ritual, a private liturgy that stills my mind before rest. I repeat the practice at the close of every day. As I step into my pyjamas, I feel the revving down of my thoughts as I relish what I know is coming: the coma of gratitude that lulls me into slumber. I consider telling Jake about it. Perhaps I might convince him to attempt a ritual of his own, a routine counting of all his blessings to relieve the chronic vexation of childlessness. They have each other, they have love. Not to mention sleep, a tidy house, and affordable vacation options. But then I stop. Jake and Sara's umbrage is a very different shape than my own; it permeates the entire landscape of their future like a dark mist. And I cannot tell them how to wade through it. I won't try to write that script. Instead, I close my eyes and picture them laughing, and choose to be thankful that I have them both in my life.

In the pre-digital era of my career in television, there used to be machines located in the station's tape library that would demagnetize old videocassettes once they were finished with, erasing all previously recorded images so that the cassettes could be reused. The process was called "bulking the tapes," waving over them with a clunky magnet the size and shape of an iron, permanently destroying old images, relegating them to memory.

The ordinance of nightly thanksgiving becomes my bulking machine, demagnetizing my mind of a day's worth of fears, worries, pressures, and daily responsibilities. A cloak of repose settles around me. I am warmed, soothed. Relief comes like fresh air in a bomb shelter.

pre-verdict jitters

Damn, it's nearly bedtime and I've only pooped three times today. I pour what feels like my eighteenth glass of water since breakfast. (Damn again. I should have been counting.)

It's the day before my follow-up appointment with the surgical oncology team, and the pH tests on my urine stream have all been yellow, light green at best. Must be stress, pre-verdict jitters, I reason. There is no earthly possible way to ingest more alkalizing vegetables than I did today, yesterday, and every day in recent memory before that. My Hungarian friend, Terry, had suggested that I try eating raw beets every day; that is how they fight cancer at home in Hungary, she assured me. I could open a Borscht restaurant with the raw beets in my refrigerator. I'm driving this cancer-fighting regimen hard; trying everything, willing it to work. Tomorrow will be my farewell appointment with the surgeon. Miles wants to give him a present, to thank him for taking all my cancer away. He wants to know what he looks like, this man who took my breast. I tell him the surgeon has grey hair, bushy eyebrows, and always wears a blue striped tie. "I'll take a picture of him for you, okay?" I'm actually looking forward to seeing him tomorrow. He is, after all, the hero of the story: tumour gone, clear margins, no spread to the lymph nodes. I want to impress him with how well my scar is healing. It is within the realm of possibility that my cancer protocol is over. The Fairy Princess said that if the pathology out of California issues me a low enough score, I might be spared chemotherapy. And the bushy-browed surgeon was pretty sure that the odds of needing radiation are quite slim.

I had heard the message, I was eating more beets and counting bowel movements. I was cancer's star pupil. Tomorrow I would get an A for good behaviour. I really was trying my absolute hardest.

———

LAST WEEK TERRY had arrived at the door with more beets, nattering in a loud voice on her cellphone. She was speaking Hungarian, apparently on a poor connection. I let her in, ignored the choppy patter, and continued about my business. A couple of times I thought I heard her mention my name, nestled in with all the unfamiliar syllables. When she hung up, Terry explained that she was speaking to a healer about trying to help me. "A healer? What kind of healer?" "An energy healer. She says she can help cure your cancer." Reason lurched inside me; survival instinct shushed its rumblings. "Go on," I said. "My sister knows this woman and she has helped a few of my sister's friends and colleagues, some of whom were told their cancer was untreatable. This woman gave them treatment and their cancer went away." The comfort of believing in the simplicity of cancer "going away," like chalk that could simply be erased from a blackboard, never to return, cannot be denied, no matter how far-fetched the explanation may seem. Then something occurred to me, and the fetchedness stretched even farther. "Wait, your sister's colleagues ... but your sister lives in Hungary. Is this woman ... in Hungary?" "Yes, but she can treat you from there, no problem. I told her about your situation last week, and today she says she has checked into your energy fields and she can treat you." I checked the flight distance between Toronto and Budapest: 7,147 kilometres. I do not understand a single syllable in Hungarian. How exactly could I be healed by a woman I had never met who was a seven-hour flight away? But the cost was minimal and Terry would broker all the arrangements. Which is how I wound up lying on my bed at 1:29 yesterday with the curtains drawn. Telephone unplugged, door closed. I was lying face up, arms by my side as instructed. The initial session was to begin at 1:30 my time. At that moment, in an office somewhere in Budapest, the Hungarian healer (I still do not know her name) would guide the forces of universal energy for one hour, targeting my left chest and underarm, destroying any remaining cancer cells, ensuring my wellness. I lay there for a moment feeling foolish. How would I explain this to the Fairy Princess? Of course, I could never tell her. Sheepishness began to set in as the cynicism of reason took hold, scolding me for wasting my time. Where is the evidence for this kind of healing? If this woman's so good, why has no one written about her in *The Lancet*, studied universal healing for the *Oncology Journal*? At the very least, I rationalized, justifying my gullible side's behaviour, I'm getting an enforced nap out of all this, lying down for an hour, regardless of whether there are invisible goblins of universal energy nibbling away at any cancer cells lingering in my left side ... My derisive musings were interrupted by the very distinct sensation of warmth and tingling under my left arm. I checked the clock. 1:32.

There are forces at work that I cannot understand—including the ones that conspired to give me cancer. As *New Yorker* writer and one-time cancer survivor Alice Trillin once wrote, "Mysticism is a cop-out, to be sure, a lateral diversion from the flat-out fear of death. But it's working. And I'm not strong enough to let it go."

moth problem

PLEASE TELL ME I'm not the only person who finds insect larvae in my dried goods. Surely other people have cooking plans interrupted when they notice that several grains of brown rice in the storage jar are in fact moving. Or uncover similar evidence of small flying creatures taking over the kitchen, such as clumps of webbing in the jar of hot pepper flakes, white wormy larvae feasting on honey stuck to the inside of the lid, and about three hundred tiny moths floating around the house for most of the summer months. Maybe I'm just lucky, health food store bulk bin shopper that I am. All I know is that my otherwise hygienic, healthy home suffers from a major moth infestation.

One particularly bad summer, my husband and I were practically knocked over when we opened the pantry cupboard doors after our vacation. It was like a scene from Alfred Hitchcock, only gutless; the moths couldn't do quite as much damage as birds—at least not to us. But they had made mincemeat out of our food supply. We threw away hundreds of dollars' worth of food: organic quinoa and spelt flour, dried fruit and maple syrup, rice and barley by the jarful. And habanero pepper powder, which my husband purchases in vast quantities, in case he ever needs to open a burrito house in a hurry. I can't get near the stuff without my eyes tearing up and succumbing to a fit of sneezes, but apparently moth sinuses are made of stronger stuff. Our half-litre keg of the Mexican fire powder was thick with webbing, a spicy love den where moths must have spent a solid month in a fiesta of procreation.

And yet, purge the devastation though we did, meticulously wiping down every surface, spritzing tea tree oil as a food-safe repellent and natural disinfectant ... the moths came back, as the old song goes. The very next day.

For most of the warm weather months, in fact, we walk around the first floor of our house clapping at the air, chasing rogue moths that take flight from the pantry to explore their new neighbourhood, having gorged themselves on our hard goods.

In winter their kitchen ranks diminish, but they migrate upward into my clothes cupboard and drawers. No amount of cedar boughs and regular laundering seems to deter them. I am waiting for the fashion magazines to feature delicate lacy detail on the front of cotton T-shirts, so that my moth-eaten wardrobe will be the height of contemporary style.

How do they get in? Some say the larvae are right there in a sack of flour or box of macaroni noodles coming home from any grocery store; other theories suggest that buying food in bulk is like giving the moths a key to your front door and a gold-embossed invitation to set up a family.

I keep thinking that if I try hard enough, I should be able to fix the problem. According to the friendly folks at howtogetridofstuff.com, I should start putting my grains and flours into the freezer for a few days after I buy them, to kill off any larvae before they can set up shop. I've been tempted to invest in a massive chest freezer and toss in every scrap of solid food that comes through the door, like some kind of anti-terrorism precautionary protocol, putting the house on amber alert against the potential threat of a moth attack.

This invasion makes me feel adversarial, a one-woman department of Homeland Security, constantly on the lookout for the origins of the problem. I keep thinking there has to be one place I can discover, one mess I must have missed. If I can just find it, I'll clear up this infestation once and for all. Ready to pounce at the discovery, I stalk the house with a constant eye out for nest Numero Uno. Looking for moth zero, the one that started it all.

I was in our third-floor bathroom one afternoon a couple of years ago, when I suddenly felt certain I had struck pay dirt. Reggie and Harper have bedrooms on the top floor of the house, where they also share a small powder room. A lavatory used exclusively by males under the age of twelve is, it must be said, quite a foul location. Not ones for flushing (nor wiping the sink after spitting toothpaste, hanging up wet towels, dropping dental floss into the wastebasket and not simply in its general vicinity) unless absolutely neces-sary, my boys had left the room in its typically slipshod condition. I was in there looking to borrow a pair of nail clippers, shuddering at the horror of my sons' hygiene stan-dards and wondering how many years it would take for them to improve, when all of a sudden I saw it. An old square-shaped wicker basket, meant to hold extra rolls of toilet paper (so one would not find oneself stranded on the john in need of bathroom tissue, three storeys up and well out of earshot from the nearest family member). That little Martha

Stewart touch must have been lost on my grade-schoolers; a few squares of toilet paper could be seen peeking out from under the basket. It was filled instead with random scraps of boyhood. Stacked on top were several back issues of *Sports Illustrated* and *The Hockey News*, stiff, warped, and bent out of shape from having been wet and left to dry on the floor. A blue sock stuck out from under the magazines, a dried brown apple core lay on top. I didn't need to guess at what else lay underneath this assortment of forgotten bits; it didn't matter. I instantly felt with complete conviction that this had to be ground zero, the place where I would find, once and for all, the mother ship of moths. All the requisite conditions were met: dampness, food, fabric, paper, and a total lack of care and attention—those creatures could have a field day in there and no one would be the wiser. I began to salivate just thinking about finally eradicating the source of our hand-clapping fervour, a giant X on my mental treasure map suddenly coming into clear view. I had finally stumbled upon it, in the one place I had never thought to look before. Now I could clear the slate, remedy the problem, restore order and domestic perfection to the family homestead.

I grabbed a washcloth from the rack, dampened it at the sink, then crouched to begin the ultimate delousing. I gingerly lifted the apple core and tossed it into the garbage. I peeled away several magazines screaming sports head-lines that were now old news, a long-abandoned colouring book, the blue sock. Working my way through the clutter, I lifted each object expecting to uncover the fountainhead of mothdom. I found a tennis ball, the missing backgammon piece, a Playmobil firefighter, and a near-empty roll of toilet paper. But there was no trace of what I was looking for: no squirming larvae, no nest webs, no dusty brown fluttering. Not a single moth.

I was so sure I had found the single source. I thought I could solve the problem right here, right now, but there is nothing for me to work with. Control slips from my eager grasp.

———

THE SURGEON HAS a lot of loose change in his pockets. Does he use a coin-operated laundromat? Have an arcade habit? For whatever reason, he is loaded with coins; he jingles them while he makes small talk with Grant. For a moment I wonder if he's nervous, but I dismiss the thought immediately. *Clear margins, contained tumour.* I remind myself of my stellar surgical results.

He also stands, I notice, with one leg pointed toward the door of the appointment room. I haven't seen him since my groggy post-surgical stupor two weeks ago; I'd forgotten how crisply his pants were pressed. His eyebrows are less bushy than I remembered. During our brief visit, his weight shifts back and forth between the leg that is committed to me and my health situation here in this moment and the leg that is anxious to move on, out the door to his next customer.

"We have a glitch."

Giddy with optimism for today's appointment, I have my camera in hand; ready to ask the surgeon to pose with me for a photo for Miles. I put the camera down now, stop thinking about the money clinking in his pleated grey pants, and downshift to what he seems to be telling me. I cannot look over at Grant; he will have gone pale at these words and blinked repeatedly, straining to understand what has just happened, the moment at which our path took a sharp, unforeseen turn.

"What's a glitch?" I ask with a half-hearted attempt at humour, my smile fading the more I look past the surgeon's tightly knotted blue silk tie and up to his face. His sharp eyes offer a whisper of sympathy to accompany this not-so-good news. The original test of my nodes, conducted while I was still under the knife, had found them to be clear. However, Dr. JinglePants explains—both legs steady, his feet pointing toward me now—the more detailed pathology, conducted after my surgery, found something. Isolated tumour cells, or ITCs, found in two of the three sentinel node sections removed during surgery. "Based on the measurements, it appears there are no more than three cancerous cells in total, in the entire sampling of lymph cells. But they're there. Cancer cells made it out from your breast tissue area and into your lymphatic system."

———

THE PICNIC HAMPER is full. Homemade sandwiches filled with mouth-watering goodness (ripe tomato and fresh basil, sharp cheddar and sliced pear) all carefully wrapped in cloth napkins; the lemonade, freshly mixed, chilling in the thermos, ice cubes clacking against the sides when it moves. Someone has brought a pie. Rhubarb? Raspberry? The feisty pink juice has burped out from a few cracks in the shell, hinting at the rich sweetness inside. Everything is in place. Hungry children and weary adults gather to begin unpacking the feast; all are ready to celebrate the simple glories of life on a summer day.

But then it rains.

Huge black clouds roll in from nowhere, unleashing a fury of wet insult on this attempt at mirth. Children squeal, parents run for cover. The picnic hamper is left on the grass, growing wet and heavy. Perfect sandwiches become bloated ruin. The bold pink of the pie juice is thinned by the rain, running in an abject dribble over the lip of the dish. The crust is wet cardboard.

The expectation of celebration is dashed, the ease of an outdoor communion stolen by a harsh turn in the weather, a shift in what was expected.

I AM DOOMED by this news. A mouthful of expletives begins to form. Humiliated that I had the temerity to bring in my camera, thinking I could cheerfully document the next chapter in my successful tour of duty through the cancer ward, I felt knocked down to size.

All my positive test results had seemed to be an evaluation of me, not just this disease. And I was doing so well. Like the good A-seeking first-born I had always been, I was sailing through all the challenges cancer dealt me thus far. I had mastered a positive attitude; kept everyone's spirits up with a calm demeanour and optimistic energy; continued to exercise and socialize right up until my surgery. Even my MRI results were impressive—single isolated tumour in one breast only, no activity in the lymph nodes. Wasn't I an impressive cancer patient? My surgery took me into A+ territory: smiled on my way into the OR, lymph system left intact. All the doctors marvelled at my super-speedy recovery—my healing was faster than the average, thank you. I was on the cancer honour roll, being sent to the front of the line for good behaviour. I had executed my recovery like a Martha Stewart recipe: neat, tidy, step-by-step until perfect results are achieved. The pleaser in me felt satiated.

ITCs.

Fuck.

I thought I scored 100 percent on my math test, and now it turns out the teacher had made a mistake. I heard a voice in my head (was it God? Was it Fate? Whoever it was, it sounded a lot like my father when he's mad at me) saying, "Now just you get back down there, Missy. Don't think you're so special. You crawl right back there in the mud because we're not finished with you yet."

I had failed to be perfect at having cancer.

The Memorial Sloan-Kettering Cancer Center in New York City is the epicentre of cutting-edge cancer research in the world. Seeing that name and logo at the top of the test results in the surgeon's hands, the bottom dropped out of my gut. The big guns were getting involved. A computer calculation conducted at Sloan-Kettering had analyzed my situation and provided a mathematical interpretation, giving us the latest word on isolated tumour cells, taking into account the patient's particulars.

My particulars: Locally Advanced cancer, Stage Two (out of four) progress, Grade Three (out of three) aggressiveness, 2.2 cm tumour with a proclivity for estrogen.

Factoring in all that with my age, the computer predicted that those three or four isolated cells in my lymph nodes indicated a 16 percent chance that there was more cancer throughout the area.

Sixteen percent. The surgeon thought that number was sufficiently high that I should undergo another surgery to remove all my lymph nodes as a precaution. He also said there is no clear answer here; different professionals would have different opinions.

Another surgery. I kept trying to turn the number over—there was an 84 percent chance that my entire lymphatic system was cancer free. I graduated high school with an 84 percent average, and that was pretty good—even my father was satisfied to see his first-born on the honour roll. Wasn't 84 percent good enough now?

I didn't want another surgery, didn't want to remove a significant chunk of the system that is the body's primary battalion in fighting future illness; the lymph nodes play a key role in the immune system.

Removing the lymph nodes also comes with another risk: the dreaded lymphedema. Caused by a blockage in the lymphatic system (which can be triggered by the removal of a large branch of that system's intricate web), lymphedema results in swelling, heaviness, tightness, aching, and recurring infections in the affected limb, which in my case would be my left arm. The threat of lymphedema was very real; I knew several women, some younger than me, who had experienced this kind of suffering after removing lymph nodes during breast cancer treatment. And here's the kicker: there is no cure. Lymphedema, should it strike, would be with me forever.

––––––

I LOOK THROUGH the notes scrawled into the journal I brought to every one of my appointments. There are tabulations of Cancer Waiting Room Math; wry observations about being the youngest person in the waiting room; comments about the sweet charity of the hospital staff; plenty of misspelled medical terms. There are also pages of questions I jotted down before appointments, important points I didn't want to forget to cover. One entry in bold capital letters fills an entire page:

WHAT PERCENTAGE OF
RISK RECURRENCE
ARE YOU GETTING ME
DOWN TO?

I wrote that one in preparation for my first session with my radiation oncologist, the third—and, I hoped, final—player in my oncological tour of duty. The California test score had indicated that chemotherapy would be of little to no benefit to my kind of cancer. One of the most potent, albeit dreaded, tools in the cancer-fighting arsenal wouldn't work for me. For the briefest of moments I envied those bald men and women slumped in the waiting room in knitted caps and headscarves. Those nameless, faceless lab technicians in California had also discovered that my cancer was aggressive as hell, and the Fairy Princess didn't like it. While she did support my disinclination for further surgery to remove the rest of my lymph nodes, she also said I would need to meet with a radiation oncologist, to explore one last option. Radiation, itself a cause of cancer, was cautiously recommended. Which was why I had scribbled down that impossible-to-answer question. If I was going to submit to the horrors and risks of five weeks of radiating my body, I wanted certainty that it would be worth it. My husband and I sat waiting in the radiation oncology appointment room, me in my patient uniform, the unflattering sickly blue cotton gown, ties at the back making it puff out around me like a cotton tent. I was trying to decide whether I looked more like a bloated fish or a pastel-blue teapot when in walked a raven-haired five-foot-ten supermodel wearing a sleek white lab coat. Definitely bloated fish.

The radiation oncologist turned out to be as brilliant and empathetic as she was beautiful. She took care to explain that I was in a grey area, between positive lymph nodes and negative, clear and unclear. Those ITCs were out there, but no one knew how many or how far they had travelled. There was, she said, no way to ever know for sure.

The ability to discover such minute wisps of cancerous activity is quite new, she assured me. I took some small, and fairly perverse, comfort in the idea that a lot of women in previous years would have sailed out of surgery thinking their lymphatic system was free of cancer when in fact these individual single cells were lurking there all along, undetectable to what was then state-of-the-art science. And I envied them their blissful ignorance.

––––––

WHAT RISKS WOULD you take if you knew there were a 16 percent chance that cancer cells could kill you? Or at least cause you more pain and suffering? I have bungee jumped off a nineteenth-century wooden rail bridge three hundred feet above a rocky river gorge, flown weightless in zero gravity with the NASA space program, eaten fried Mopani worms in South Africa, given birth to three children without getting any genetic tests or even ultrasounds to confirm their physical well-being. I am not averse to a reasonable amount of risk.

Leaving my lymph nodes intact meant they could continue to protect me for the rest of my life as a vital aspect of my immune and circulatory systems; it also meant there was a risk that rogue cancer cells were making their way through that same circulatory system.

So my question for the supermodel oncologist was simple, written in capital letters taking up an entire page as evidence of its volume in my mind, its urgency in my heart, the desperation with which it was asked: WHAT PERCENTAGE OF RISK RECURRENCE ARE YOU GETTING ME DOWN TO?

I wanted the mathematical evidence that radiation was worth the undertaking, an assurance that the 16 percent chance that cancer cells were somewhere else in my body would have the stuffing kicked out of it and flattened to a couple of measly zeroes. I wanted a number, a hard, solid snatch of proof that I would be okay. I wanted to know I could control the outcome by making the right choice.

———

I SAT FOR A LONG TIME in that untidy bathroom, turning the stray backgammon piece over and over in my hand.

There is no secret spot that holds the key to my moth problem. No single source, no one hidden nook where I can swoop in, sterilize, and solve the problem forever.

I mused at the futility of trying to make everything Just So. We carry the illusion that if we can just find the key, the ticket to happiness, all will be well. The right job, the right brand of product, the right address, the right hairdo; will that do it? The right cancer treatment.

But there is no single action, single decision, single

discovery that makes everything make sense and establishes any lasting suggestion of harmony and order in this life. There are just a lot of choices. Each one of them seems to be the one that holds the clue to the hiding place where all the moths are coming from.

I put the backgammon piece in my pocket, hoping I'd remember to return it to the game board it is part of and not run it through the laundry in my pants pocket. I slowly replaced the magazines, books, and action figures. Why do I work so hard searching for the key to make everything right? There is no key. And what's more, it dawned on me then, there is no right.

the earth without me

THAT SNOW BLOWER on sale at the hardware store is the model gadget: convenient, affordable, and lifestyle enhancing. The drudgery of a long Canadian winter seems more manageable with the prospect of a handy, fossil fuel–burning motorized device to tackle the driveway after every snowfall. So how unpopular is the environmentalist for pointing out that your snow-removing machine's noxious emissions contaminate the air we breathe, its offshore-made plastic parts will soon be rendered obsolete and clog a landfill, and the world would be better off if you cleared your sidewalk with a shovel? That is, by environmental terms, the *right* way to clear snow.

Snow blower, electric can opener, no-iron sheets, automatic baby-wipe warmer ... There is a device to make every aspect of our lives easier, faster, more under control, available at bargain prices a short combustion-engine ride away at the retail outlets now standing in place of wilderness and farmland. So why, many of us reason, shouldn't we acquire each of these gadgets, one in every colour? The sustainability argument can be a tough sell in the modern world. Swimming upstream is exhausting, as contemporary environmentalists are not the first to experience.

In 1787, enslaving another human being was *de rigeur*; the convenience, affordability, and lifestyle-enhancing attributes of owning a slave could not be denied. A growing dependence on sugar, the new must-have item of the time, kept the slave trade operating at a hum—*somebody* had to do the back-breaking work to harvest the cane. Human appetite dictated cultural and social norm. Which is likely why the groups who opposed slavery and lobbied to see it banished were small in number and unpopular in their message. Early Quakers were among the most vocal abolitionists; in many ways their anti-slavery efforts parallel the modern-day environmental movement. Trying to convince the masses to give up conveniences to which they feel entitled, basing the argument on vague morality (or science, equally intangible), is an unpopular and uphill battle. Abraham Lincoln said, "If slavery is not wrong, nothing is wrong." And yet it has taken several generations to shift global culture away from an utterly inhumane practice. There were lots of colourful characters among the colonial Quakers; irreverent and outspoken, they paraded around in shackles and chains, held public rants and other stunts they felt would be most effective to influence the anti-slavery agenda. But the most vigorous and obstreperous players in the drama wound up dying young, their angry, frustrated protest not sustainable over the long term.

The Civil War era's sugar is today's oil—the addiction none of us is willing to break, regardless of the social or environmental cost. Like the Quakers before them, environmentalists operate outside the mainstream, drawing attention to the injustice behind many of our conveniences, sputtering with indignation. If you're not outraged, they argue, you're not paying attention. Tooker Gomberg paid outraged attention to environmental and social injustices for a living. A passionate social activist in Canada, he wrote books and articles, started community bike organizations, ran for public office in Edmonton and Toronto on a platform of sustainability and social justice. With every rousing speech, every thought-provoking article, every pedal of his bike through city traffic, he exuded hope for a clean, green society and championed the finer points of his vision every day to all and any who would listen. Then, in 2004, Tooker Gomberg jumped off the Angus L. Macdonald Bridge in Halifax, Nova Scotia, ending a life that had been spent mostly in fervent protest against ecological crises. I say mostly because for the final two years of his life he lived out of the limelight, largely lying in bed, trapped in a deep state of depression. In what was meant to be a private exercise for his therapist during that dark time, he penned a letter that has since become a very public tool within the activist community. Written on Earth Day 2002, Gomberg's "Letter to an Activist" describes how he *"lived, breathed and focused on activism. It kept me thinking, inspired, interested and alive."* He goes on to describe how all-consuming his activism became, how his perspective grew too narrow, leaving no room for the many other pleasures of a full life. Appearing to take stock of the journey down his own Secret Path, he wrote, *"Maybe I was living in a bubble of naiveté, doing my own thing, unconcerned that my perspectives and actions were so different from 'normal.'"*

———

MY SECOND-FAVOURITE photograph of Miles was taken at a rally to support the ratification of the Kyoto Protocol. Not quite three, wearing a hand-me-down ski jacket and a lopsided, ill-fitting toque (there are no Just So outfits for third-borns; they are chronically outfitted in castoffs), he holds a wooden stake bearing a placard with the words "Hummers Suck" written in bold capital letters. The stake was clearly too heavy for his toddler strength; the sign is crooked over his head. I must have put the prop in his hands for the photo, to create for posterity the appearance of a politicized preschooler. Once the camera was put away, though, I'm sure he dropped the sign and began to ask for snacks. Kyoto assemblies notwithstanding, I was never what you'd call an environmental activist cliché: sporting hemp drawstring pants and unshaven armpits, carrying a suckling five-year-old in a sling at every protest rally against big oil and corporate greed. I love those folks, and I envy them their clarity. But I can't be like them—for one thing, I find hemp pants too itchy. I have never tied myself to a tree, never faced down a bulldozer, and never been arrested (unless you count my lead foot and its uncanny magnetism for radar speed traps). My voice, not my body, has been the tool of environmental expression, and the expression is one of resolution, not tribulation. Follow me, I dared to suggest, and I will show you a better way, for a healthier world. What I want is for those activists' values—mindful living and sustainable consumption—to be mainstream, not relegated to subcultures and protest rallies. I want to live in a world where healthy decisions are easy to make and don't require a second mortgage. I want my children to grow up informed and educated about the ingredients in their food, the chemicals in their cleaning products, the safety of what's in their bathroom cabinet, and the impact their decisions have on the health of the planet. But for reasons I don't quite understand, that's an exhausting sell. And I don't feel up to the role of missionary at the moment.

Newspapers are spread across the breakfast table each morning, weighty with reports of crisis and despair. Species are erased from botanists' charts. There are now more obese people in the world than there are starving people. Environmental legislation is dismantled in favour of easier, faster business development. The breast milk I had been so sure was the right choice for my babies scientists now say is loaded with toxins from every fume I ever inhaled from paint thinner to car exhaust. Headlines like these appear to be written in Greek; I am not able to process the information. The earth operates without me now; no part of my energy can be spared for global concerns. The cacophony of disaster fades to a distant hum.

My world view is shrinking. Raspberries from Venezuela and goji berries from Fiji are soaked in petroleum, as local food advocates like to say, having racked up so many greenhouse gas emissions on their journey to the North American plate. But they're also loaded with cancer-fighting antioxidants. When I got sick I started buying them. Lots of them. I used to agonize that people might wander past my house on recycling day and judge me for having bought the occasional carton of non-organic milk. There are extremists in every movement; all I wanted was to shrink my footprint and help others do the same. Now I'm wondering if I didn't make my footprint too small: living such a circumscribed life, stepping so tightly within the bounds of environmental do-goodery. My own bubble of naiveté. What has happened to my desire to save the earth? I spend every day just trying to save myself. Part of the inherent message in the conservation movement is to be less selfish, more magnanimous towards the earth and other people, not so focused on our own needs and wants. But a cancer diagnosis deals a sharp blow to the ability to think globally. Right now I think about the earth without me.

David Servan-Schreiber's *Anticancer* book bursts with research showing that inner repose is critical to long-term health. The rhythmic patterns of the autonomous nervous system—heart rate, blood pressure, respiration—become synchronized during meditation and the repetition of the rosary. This harmonization of biological rhythms is associated with a number of health benefits: improved functioning of the immune system, reduction of inflammation, and superior regulation of blood-sugar levels: the three main factors that act against the development and growth of cancer cells.

The science confirms what the body knows instinctively: practising meditation, living a life of gratitude and peacefulness, focusing on the positive—this is the anti-cancer lifestyle. And being told you have cancer is something one should only ever have to endure once.

The genomic analysis conducted through the clinical trial in California tells me that there is a 13 percent chance that my cancer will come back over the next ten years, provided that I continue with adjuvant drug therapy over that time. (But has California talked to Sloan-Kettering in New York? Does the 13 percent know about the 16 percent?)

The Fairy Princess assures me that radiation will reduce recurrence risk, and we can shave a few more percentage points off with different drug treatments—one that will shut down my estrogen supply, another that will block cancer's receptors, yet another to strengthen my bone marrow. And who knows? Maybe I can knock off another percentage point or two with all those raw beets. Regardless of how brilliant the care of my oncology team, my own gut tells me that abandoning my desire to control the world, the future, the environment, will be the best treatment of all. Considering the uncertain odds I will now live with every day, isn't it ironic that I should feel a burdensome weight lifted from my shoulders at the very thought? Yet the idea of living with less judgment is a potent physic, the heady elixir of approbation. So where does that leave my desire to protect the earth? How do I balance my passion to preserve the natural world I love with the need to protect my own health? How do I do battle with the forces that sabotage our planet and at the same time live a life that is as stress-free as possible? Accept. Live in the moment. Be. This is cancer's teaching. It must be the message I am meant to hear. But how can that be reconciled with corporate lobby tactics, chemical contaminants in baby products, algae blooms, species at risk, and boil-water advisories? How do you live a long and healthy life and still preach the eco-gospel? What does that look like? If environmental activism is not about judging the right vs. wrong way to make dinner or get to work or take out the garbage, then what else might it be? No doubt the work needs doing and the message bears repeating, but at what personal cost? What does it take to wage the battle? I wonder if poor health is the price of protest.

After spending his life paying outraged attention, Tooker Gomberg wrote, *"Maybe my brain is poisoned from so much thinking about tragic ecological issues, pondering bad air, and getting frustrated at the slow rate of improvement and the rapid destruction of the living world."* Two years after that writing, he was dead at forty-eight.

grounded

I STAND NEAR the edge of a large, crowded room with fuzzy, cream-coloured walls. Faceless characters surround me, their words a blur, their bodies stuttering through jerky motions, like robots running on low batteries. Here is my high school biology teacher, talking with the dental hygienist from last week's appointment, and there is the friendly young man who stops by each month to read our gas meter. The question of how they know each other does not come up.

Something on the other side of the room catches my interest, a wave, an idea, the promise of something better, so I move to get to it. But I do not elbow my way through the crowd of robots; neither do I skirt the perimeter of the space. Instead, I lift my heels off the ground, feel my body's full weight transfer to my toes and forefoot, then spring upward into the air. Wisps of someone's hair tickle my knees and shins as I skirt the hairlines and foreheads of the people standing near me; my body swings and lifts into a horizontal pose above their heads, beyond their reach. Without effort, I lie parallel to the floor, floating above the crowd as though suspended in water. To manoeuvre, I reach forward with pointed fingers and pull the air back with a commanding motion, sweeping a heart shape with my hands, directing the air down toward my hips, propelling my body forward; behind me, my legs bend and whip like a bullfrog traversing the pond. Swimming an airborne breaststroke, I levitate across the room, easy as you please. Without so much as a pinch of fairy dust, nor the hard work of Peter Pan's youth-obsessed meditations, I can fly.

The efficiency of flying pleases me; never before has travel been so expedient. Hovering out of the way of inconvenient congestion, I travel a wide-open plane, ripe with possibility. There is power in weightlessness, an effortless might.

Some people fly like birds, but only in their dreams. I've never experienced the soaring perspective of the hawk first-hand while sleeping, never rocked along the aerial swoops and dives of a swallow. I can only imagine the rush and glory of coasting beneath the clouds when I hear friends describe a flying dream. But on more occasions than I can count, I have used this humbler flight pattern as a delightful means of locomotion to get where I need to go. This low-level flight-swim skill is a gift; I realize not many other people can do it, but I don't abuse the blessing.

———

I MUST SHEEPISHLY CONCEDE that it was quite recently that I realized I can only fly in my dreams. I actually believed I could do it anytime, even awake. For longer than I care to admit, I lived with the easy certainty that I was always only a foot flex away from leaping upward to air-swim across the room, the parking lot, the grocery store. So clear is the sensation in my mind, so certain I am about which muscles to fire in which sequence to achieve lift, that I still marvel, forsaken, at the disappointing reality that no one but the congregation of random acquaintances in a dreamscape scraped up from my subconscious will ever bear witness to the delightful feat I thought I had mastered. The very thought of being permanently grounded leaves me bereft; I really did think I could fly.

rumblings of emergent faith

I WONDER ABOUT the strangers in California who have dissected my tumour and declared that it will not respond to chemotherapy ... are they surfers on weekends? Do they sit in traffic on their way to the lab, staring out the car window at the Hollywood sign? It is aggressive cancer, their genomic analysis suggests, and there is a 13 percent chance it will come back. They seem to know this for certain.

Other strangers in a New York City lab (do they take their children to FAO Schwarz on weekends? Jog in Central Park?) argue there is a 16 percent chance that cancer spread into my lymphatic system before my breast was removed. They too have applied decisive mathematics to the quandary.

Dr. JinglePants insists the best way to reduce that risk is to remove the rest of my lymph nodes. He knows what he knows; the surgeon recommends surgery to ensure my future wellness.

The Fairy Princess says no surgery is required.

The raven-haired supermodel says radiation would be prudent.

They, too, seem convinced.

Who do I believe? Where do I put my faith? And how will I ever know if my decision was the right one?

———

THE FIRST THING I noticed was the tulips; tops snapped off, their stalks stood at attention in the flowerbed, pale green knitting needles in the dirt. As the car pulled into the driveway, I took in the shabby stucco bungalow, the vinyl windows, white plastic railing, and the remains of the tulips, wondering what force of nature had interrupted spring's longing and robbed those scrawny stems of their colourful bling. Windstorm? Gluttonous squirrel? I wondered too how this humble residence in a remote corner of a Toronto suburb could possibly house all the majesty and healing power that had been promised to me. I had been brought here to see The Master; could this unimpressive, untended garden really herald the great panacea? For all the intensity and urgency of its initial diagnosis, cancer is a battle waged in slow motion, complete with extended waiting periods between treatments. As I bided my time healing from surgery and awaiting the onset of radiation, my friends Ayumi and Hiro had arranged this appointment. A young Japanese couple, they are both shiatsu therapists. Weekend mornings, Hiro was studying qi gong, Chinese energy healing, at a Chinese community centre north of the city. He was learning to channel universal energy through meditation and transfer it to patients to make them well, training with a man both he and Ayumi referred to only as The Master. "We showed The Master your photograph," Ayumi had told me when she tentatively suggested I try qi gong treatments as complementary cancer care therapy. (If there are any universals to the cancer experience, the friendly suggestion of ways to complement your treatment has to be one of them.) "My photograph?" "Yes, The Master needs to see if someone is a good person before he agrees to treat them. He says he will see you." I assumed she had shown him the photograph on the cover of my first book, a promotional shot for a television show I had hosted. I had never liked that photograph with its over-coiffed hair and glittery jewellery, feigned sophistication that had been plastered all over billboards and bus shelters across the country; it never really felt like the real me. I wondered if The Master would be expecting someone more glamorous. But I was intrigued, and once again tempted, by the promise of powerful, painless healing. So I agreed to come along and meet The Master.

A short, hunched, and balding man stands inside the door of the bungalow. His jowls are wrinkled, his clean-shaven skin occasionally interrupted by a rogue, white, two-inch hair. His eyes are small, his mouth wide. He is a Chinese Yoda. Whatever benevolent qualities he ascribed to me by virtue of my photograph, they are not sufficient to merit spoken communication. Thwarting my chirpy, WASPy-mannered attempts at polite greetings, The Master simply grunts, directing me to remove my shoes and sit down in the living room. The small space contains three pieces of furniture: an L-shaped couch along the windows, with a view of the broken tulips; a small stool; and an altar. I take a seat on the stool, trying to take in all the detail on the shrine. It is decked out like a mall at Christmastime, chock-a-block with colourful wares. There are two porcelain cats standing in profile, front paws held aloft; vases of bamboo; photographs of Chinese spiritual leaders; gold bowls filled with red paper;

parchment paper hangings covered with Chinese characters; a plate covered with oranges. I am a tourist here, marvelling at the surfaces, ignorant of the meaning behind the icons. There is tremendous spiritual commitment attached to this display, but it does not move my heart; I don't know what any of it means.

The skin around my scar is itchy, a sign that my white blood cells have begun to patch and repair the damage; restoring calm to my severed chest. I reach gingerly inside my shirt and delicately scratch the skin near my armpit, but the entire area is numb so I experience none of a good scratch's customary relief. I cannot feel a thing. It occurs to me that I'm treating this experience as a lark, a benign whimsical approach to getting better; if it has actual healing benefit, so much the better. I can't begin to comprehend the depth of this man's faith, nor can I be sure whether to believe in it. If I don't believe, then why am I here? Do all cancer patients take a crack at alternative therapies to supplement their conventional treatment? Or just the ones who desperately seek to maintain control? "What happened to your lower back?" The Master, hands resting lightly on my backside, had to repeat his question a few times before I could understand it. "I'm sorry? My lower back? No, there's nothing the matter with my back." Hadn't Hiro explained my condition, which part of my body I was here to cure?

"It's my breast. Cancer—" I suddenly felt foolish being here.

But The Master ignored me, insisting there was hot energy radiating from my lower back on my left side, near my butt cheek—surely I could explain why? I tried several times to convince him that he was off the mark, my doubt in this exercise growing by the minute. Finally, I began to raise my voice. "I have never had a back injur—oh, wait a minute!" I paused. Dim recollections of a rainy day fall onto concrete, landing on my lower back. "I had a bad fall, a hematoma on my bottom. Terrible bruise ... but it went away. It's fine now." That injury had happened years ago. Yet The Master had pinpointed it exactly, with no visible clues or physical evidence of pain—a crushing blow to my skepticism. I felt the rumblings of emergent faith. Hiro, the devoted student, had been observing the Master's movements, the position of his hands on various points on my body. Now he stood and retrieved the water bottles we had brought with us. Checking first for The Master's permission, he asked me to sip from each of the bottles, my stainless steel refillable thermos and the disposable plastic one he had bought at the gas station on the way here. I drank from each bottle—was this part of a ritual?—and handed them back to Hiro. He bent briefly in supplication before placing both bottles on the colourful shrine. The Master moved toward the altar, also stopping to pray as he approached. He held his index finger above each bottle, pointing down into the open tops, occasionally circling the air above the rims. Hiro whispered something to me about looking at the air above the bottle openings. I strained to make out the energy passing between man and water, hoping to spot the kind of wiggly air you can see across the top of the toaster just before the morning slices pop up, but I couldn't see anything moving except The Master's finger. He bowed again to the shrine, then picked up the water bottles and passed them to me. Hiro motioned for me to take another drink. The water tasted completely different. Fear of leaving this imperfect planet knocks me flat. Perhaps it has also addled my judgment.

For thirty more minutes, as Hiro looked on studiously, The Master crouched in silence behind me, beside me, holding his hands an inch away from various parts of my body. He touched me only once, for the big finale, when he whacked my back in an up-and-down pattern, so hard I noisily sputtered lungfuls of air into the otherwise quiet room.

Afterward, I thanked The Master for his help and walked down the front steps toward the car. As I sat in the back seat waiting for Hiro and Ayumi, I noticed the afternoon sun casting shadows of the tulip stalks across the earth in the flowerbed. My entire body felt warm, as though I'd been lying in the sun myself. But my head spun, trying to make sense of what had just happened.

———

CAN FAITH REALLY HEAL? Or is it a panacea for those of us desperate for control of *something*? There is so much I want to be able to dissect, to understand clearly, and yet which cannot be explained in words that make sense to me. If there are energetic forces at work behind the scenes, why did they give me cancer? And why won't they help Jake and Sara have a baby? How can I have faith that such an unbalanced universe is unfolding as it should?

ding ding ding

IT WAS DECIDED by the raven-haired supermodel oncologist that radiation would be prudent in light of the extremely aggressive classification of my cancer. Radiation is basically highly targeted X-ray zapping, applied every day over an extended period of time—a protocol designed to sanitize the area where the cancer was present (chest wall) and where it might possibly be present (lymph nodes), destroying any leftover or stray cells that slipped out the back door before my surgery. Thus began the monotonous rhythm of my summer. For five weeks I took my daily communion with Primus 5, one of six radiation machines at the cancer centre, tireless workhorses dishing out nuclear medicine to an endless stream of patients. The routine goes like this: Get to the hospital every weekday morning at the appointed time. Swipe my health card to let the system know I have arrived. Wait to be called into the treatment area. Change into bloated-fish ensemble: the unbecoming pale blue gown, ties at the back. Pore over back issues of *Vogue*, marvelling at the fashion trends I missed back in Fall 2007. Wonder what fashion trends are unfolding this season in the world beyond these blue-gowned hospital halls.

Get called in to the zapping room. Untie the gown, lie on my back on a metal table, raise my left arm into a support over my head. Lie perfectly still while two technicians peel back the gown and position the machinery to line up with the six tattoo marks on my chest wall. Listen as they confirm the measurements: Floor height? 16.1 Tattoo span? 16.5 Shift? 1 centimetre. Wonder what the numbers mean. Try not to laugh as they outline each of the tattoos with a Sharpie marker (it tickles). Try not to cry listening to the music they play on the boombox—Gino Vannelli, April Wine, and Lionel Richie's "Three Times a Lady."

Watch the giant China Syndrome machine rotate in a huge arc around me, roughly two feet away from my body, as they program its four positions for my treatment. The raven-haired supermodel and her team of technicians have isolated the exact areas to target from a variety of angles so that my chest gets the full hit of radiation, my lung gets just a little, and my heart hopefully not any. The zapping is emitted from a little patch of light. Each day when I arrive, the whirligigs inside the China Syndrome machine spin until they reveal the precise shape of light that has been programmed for the specific target area on my body. The weird thing is that the shape of the beam is almost an exact replica of the property assessment map of my Toronto home. I'm not kidding. (For a second or two during my initial session, I wondered whether they did that for everyone: send out a radiation beam that matches the floor plan of the place they live. My brain was too swamped with new information to think straight.)

Then I listen for the routine "ding-ding-ding," the signal that the machine is in place and the nice technicians who do not have cancer and sure don't want to get it are leaving the zapping room so that they can be at a safe remove when they press the button to unleash the beast.

The radiation beam itself is invisible (believe me, I've looked hard) and painless, at least so far. The machine beaming it makes a hilarious noise, which I imagine as a drunken sailor who is running out of breath while playing a kazoo, or possibly an oboe with a plastic drinking straw stuck in its bell. These are tedious, repetitive visits. I do what I can to liven things up.

After four rounds of the inebriated sailor, my technician friends come in and tell me I can go. A few different technicians rotate on a schedule; so far my favourites are Batu the Mongolian radiator and Vicky the radiator who lives on a farm and asks me questions about where she should recycle Styrofoam. I'm trying to get Batu to bring in some Mongolian music (I figure how much worse can it be than April Wine?).

I am not allowed to shave my left armpit, nor use deodorant on it. I'm not supposed to use very hot water in the shower and have to avoid rubbing the area with soap. This is to protect the skin taking a beating from the beams. Approach me from the left and you'll recognize the distinct odour of a construction worker on overtime. The trick to radiation treatments is to lie utterly inactive so that the beams land on the targeted area only, punishing any rogue ITCs as intended, and not healthy lung tissue. The exacting measurements delineated by my tattoo marks are checked and rechecked to the millimetre with callipers before each treatment; the accuracy of the beam can be thrown off by a simple deep breath or a clenched muscle. Alone in the dark room I lie, supine, in a tranquil state for twenty minutes at a time every day, week after week after week. Strangely, I'm learning to like it. Not the part with the gamma-ray death beam firing into my flesh, but the forced hush; clemency for each day. I am becoming an expert at stillness. Each round quiets me further into a kind of bizarre peace, the ultimate liberation. Pinned under a hazardous death ray meant to save my life, I am trapped into submission.

At the end of each session Velcro straps are ripped open, releasing my radiated self back into the day. I ball up the powder blue gown and toss it into a receptacle, gingerly pull clothing back on over increasingly seared flesh, and don my helmet for the trip home. Walking past crowds of withered sick people wearing a bicycle helmet is my bird-flip to cancer; you haven't got all of me, not yet.

The cancer centre is situated at the top of a hill, the northernmost rise at the end of the city's longest ravine. The trees that filter sunlight into the centre's high windows are one small part of an expansive forest running down the hill behind the hospital grounds, alongside a river, through a network of parks and valleys. Yet another kindness, showered upon me by friends with minivans, is a ride to my treatments each day with my bicycle in tow, ferrying me up the hills leading to the hospital so that I can coast home on two wheels. It is my favourite part of the day.

As I swoop downhill onto the network of trails running south through the ravine, cancer-ward blues evaporate under the summer sun. The ride is breezy, head-clearing. Trees, grasses, and a sparkling brook soften my thoughts away from the stark, beige machinery of my morning, soaking up fear like a sponge. My rattletrap Mary Poppins bike clanks like a cutlery tray over every bump and crack, while serious cyclists on speedy racers whiz past at twice my speed. As the treatments wear on, my speed slows even further. The deep breaths I try to take, head cocked back to salute a blue sky, grow more difficult each week.

By Day 16 it looks as though I have taken a long nap in the Mexican midday sun. My chest is now covered in something less recognizable as human skin and more like a hideous red explosion of hellfire. Lord Voldemort himself is poised to erupt from my armpit.

Gamma rays course through me; I imagine I glow in the dark while sleeping. Which is what I do most of the day once I'm home from the hospital. The boys race past me up what feels more like a mountain than a staircase; my legs are lead shafts, bearing the weight of my cinder-block torso. Must. Lie. Down.

Every day that goes by, a little more of my fortitude slips away. My bicycle remains locked in the yard. I try to rally some punch, but it's like holding smoke in a shoebox; eventually I lift the lid and it's gone. The zealotry machine was the first thing to shut down.

carousel of chaos

OVER THE COURSE of five weeks of radiation and the multiple medical appointments that accompanied the treatment, I caught up on all the back issues of a lot of women's magazines. Whenever Primus 5 or the Fairy Princess were running behind schedule, I boned up on the at-home spa manicure, took mental notes on the top five relationship myths, and learned why I shouldn't diet for my high school reunion. Usually I flipped past the advertisements, disregarded the two-breasted Models of Perfection taunting my middle-age complacency, mocking my best efforts at style, posing as my (and every other hard-working, dish-washing, sleep-deprived woman's) preferable self, reaping the purported benefits of whatever snack, lotion, or feminine hygiene product they hold gingerly in those skeletal digits. But one day, in one magazine, like a kindred spirit found at an otherwise uncomfortable social gathering, one advertisement leapt through the barrage of pretty-faced propaganda and registered meaning. Selling a packaged, processed convenience food that I would never actually buy, it stopped my robotic page turning and reeled in my interest immediately.

In this particular advertisement, there are no Photo-shopped figurines, no plasticized people pitching better living. Lifestyle is implied in words alone. The entire page is filled with text, in 8-point type. No capital letters, no sentences, no hawking headline. Except for a remarkably small photograph of the packaged food item placed in the centre of the page, the ad is simply a sequence of noted tasks in a list, a run-on stream-of-consciousness tally of to-do's.

"... call plumber to fix garburator, finalize sales projec-tions, take kids to swimming lesson, drink eight glasses of water, rotate the tires, find my umbrella, research our summer vacation, read up on current events, organize music playlists, find Nana's postal code, schedule sales meeting, replace batteries in camera, practise public speaking, donate old clothes, take a pottery class, upload photos of kids, replace vacuum cleaner bag, explain to Molly how birds fly ..."

It continues on like this across the entire page. The list has no beginning and no end; it appears to continue long before and long after what we see on the page. Like the to-do list each one of us carries around—scrawled on the back of an envelope, typed meticulously into an electronic data collector, or tallied mentally—it is endless.

Smack in the centre of this sea of worries is the simple image of the packaged food being advertised—a shortcut to dinner prep, presumably, in the midst of all these other things to do.

Connection strikes like a bat to the head. I recognize the state of mind, had thought I was unique in my mania, but this ad proves otherwise. The modern overachieving working mother's chronic frenzy must be universal. There are expect-ations to be met, some determined by a job description,

others self-imposed. Like my mother before her, Martha
Stewart makes lists, monthly calendars of garden prepara-
tions, craft projects, and meal plans; we feel we should too.
Gretchen Rubin sold a gazillion copies of *The Happiness
Project* by compiling cumulative monthly strategies for
tidying, de-cluttering and list making. ("Every Wednesday
is List Day!") Somehow my generation has interpreted the
pioneering strides of our bra-burning forebears as a call to
master both the professional success of our hard-working
fathers and the domestic do-goodery of our hard-working
mothers, without adding any extra hours to the clock.
Allison Pearson skewered the modern woman's juggle in her
bestselling book *I Don't Know How She Does It*, so clearly
we've noticed the condition and all its perils. But it hasn't
slowed us down. We may be able laugh at the caricature of
ourselves ... but still we race along. There are people to be
looked after, needs to be tended. From the domestic to the
professional, we amass lists of requirements, tabulations of
tasks to move us forward, onward to that stage of accomplished perfection we reach ... when, exactly? And I wonder
just how many of the items on our bottomless list have to be
scratched off before we arrive? And what would that state
of perfection look like when we get there? Never mind, let's
just keep working toward it, whatever it is.

"Busy as a one-armed paper hanger" is how a friend
used to describe my pre-cancer life. Busy is the modern
epidemic. If idle hands are the devil's tools, most post-
millennial North American citizens are practically Puritans,
so seldom are our hands, minds, or any other body part
resting in neutral. Higher costs of living, unsteady econ-
omies, women's liberation—we've heard all the reasons why

the typical two-income household has come to be as frantic and fast-paced as the stock exchange trading floor just before the closing bell. But we have become so accustomed to living with constant purpose, objectives, and plans, we may not have noticed how taxing it is to live this way. Or we notice, but aren't sure what to do about it.

There is no social stigma attached to the frenzy, no peer motivation to slow us down. Rather it is the opposite; busy is popular currency, traded among members of modern society like a precious commodity. Busy is the silkiest cloth at the emporium, the most well-travelled spice. Living with a full schedule speedily typed into a pinging, vibrating mobile device is a highly valued state of being. And, as with any addiction, it becomes self-perpetuating. We feel a rush from being in a rush; we take pride in the breakneck pace at which we travel through our days.

Being busy is a competitive sport. Greetings between friends and neighbours resemble nothing so much as sparring contests, exchanged comparisons of busy-ness. A simple, "How was your weekend?" can yield a full two-minute tally of birthday parties attended, errands run, workouts completed, sporting events watched, and in-laws hosted.

It happens in the workplace, in the park, in the grocery store.

Busy A: "Hey, how's it going? I haven't seen you in a while!"

Busy B: "Oh, my gosh, I know. Things have been just crazy, I am so busy you can't imagine. My work is nuts right now."

Busy A, picking up dropped gauntlet: "Yeah, same here. Johnny has hockey three nights a week because he's playing rep this year, and Brenda started soccer so I had to run out and get her soccer cleats last night after work because we just realized her old ones don't fit, but meanwhile my presentation to my boss was due this morning, so I was up all night finishing that ... plus it's Johnny's birthday next week so I've got to plan his whole party. Oh my god, I'm stressed just thinking about it."

Busy B sees A's busy and raises, speaking at breakneck speed while retreating backwards, to reinforce the urgency of Things To Get Done other than this conversation: "Wow, yeah, well I just took over the entire sales division so I've got like twenty-two people reporting to me now—it's nuts. And my mother-in-law isn't well, so we're in and out of the hospital all the time. We're just go-go-go these days ..."

Except it's never just "these days"; it's most of the time.

Why are we so married to that endless to-do list, rushing headlong from one accomplishment to another? Because modern society itself is set to a rapid tempo; we suffer from what James Gleick, author of *Faster: The Acceleration of Just About Everything*, calls "hurry sickness." We can spend all night on the dizzying merry-go-round of social media, caught in an avalanche of opinion and news; at any hour of the day we can find updates on global events from the financial to the political; stock trading and work habits and nutrition and sex lives and child rearing are discussed, analyzed, taught in courses. There are more life coaches and fewer jobs, more gadgets and time-saving devices and yet ever-increasing demands on our time, more aspirational TV shows and magazines laying out the must-follow steps for design harmony and domestic order amidst the roiling sea of contemporary chaos. Ergo the boasting, advertising all that we have on our plates, like so many circus performers trying to outdo each other with more and more balls in the air. You may be able to juggle three tennis racquets and a boomerang, but I can do six spatulas, two steak knives, and the soup tureen from the good china. And please note my stylish new boots.

I can over-schedule and multi-task right up there with the best of them; my father used to say I was "burning the candle at both ends." My first-born need to achieve is deeply wired; the desire to get somewhere other than right here. I know how easy it is to believe that the condition we'll be in at the bottom of that list, with each of the items scratched off in satisfying completion, holds the promise of being better than where we are at the top of the list, with the looming task of having to actually accomplish it.

But what if there were no list? That's what it looks like to have cancer.

A cancer diagnosis is a searing hot poker; pesky, flimsy demands on one's time instantly wither and recede. It provides burning clarity on what matters and what doesn't. It knocks a showy to-do list down to a single priority: Stay. The Fuck. Alive.

Even after a cancer diagnosis, a first-born's instincts take some time to reprogram—the overachiever doesn't give up without a fight. In those first stunned days after the news, I panicked and cried at the stress of having to return every phone call, fretted over how to fit those speaking engagements in between MRI appointments. I compared myself to other cancer patients I know who worked through their treatment, thinking I could be doing more, and doing it better.

Not for the first time, my husband talked some sense into me.

"Listen, it doesn't matter if you had a previous commitment or if you have to leave a few phone calls unanswered. All that matters right now is that you rest and get better. Honour what the hell is going on in your body and forget about everything else."

The ultimate gift for the busy working mother, especially one who has assigned herself to clean up the earth: permission to check out. So I stepped off the carousel of chaos, and for the first time in my life, stopped feeling that I had to accomplish anything more than a low-acidity salad and a nap. It was a curious novelty, to wipe the slate clean; other than the roughly three hundred appointments each week, I wasn't sure what could possibly rise up to fill my schedule.

a period of silence

I NEVER DID RETRACE my steps back up that hill. Following my nose, taking my cues from smaller patches of trilliums I continued to see along the route (though none, to this day, as massive and spectacular as that first roadside prize), I just kept going. Pedal, breathe, gaze, admire, hydrate, pedal, enjoy. Repeat. I stopped trying to figure out the most efficient, best route back; instead, I simply meandered, and found a new path back to where I'd started. It took a little huffing and puffing up a few smaller hills, but none so steep and endless as the one I'd sailed down. I took a tally of my circumstances—strong legs, blue sky, spring's grassy scent, whimsical breeze—and it fuelled each pedal stroke. If I went back to that part of the countryside today, I'd never be able to recreate that return trip route; details and directions have been completely erased from my mind. Each spring since, I have thought of returning with my children and husband, to show them the trilliums that gave me such hope. But I have no idea where I found them; I only know how they found me, when joy trumped responsibility.

WITH TALISMANS OF HOPE, love, and strength lined up along a small wooden bench in my bedroom, I light a beeswax candle. I sit comfortably in front of the makeshift shrine with my legs crossed, and I begin to breathe deeply. I have never been too clear on how to meditate. My chatterbox personality has always kept the air filled with sound so that I haven't had too many extended periods of silence within which to experiment with the concept. But if there is ever a time to attempt to reign in the gallivanting mind, it is during cancer treatment. This modest ritual disciplines my whirling mind to a period of silence. No to-do list to distract me— my to-do list right now has only one thing on it: get well. My exhausted body is forgotten, as is my crispy-fried skin and the remaining days of lying under the danger beams. I cannot think of the world, take its pulse, manage its patterns, or assume responsibility for it. I am simply a part of it.

Outside my bedroom window, the leaves make patterns of movement in the wind, a monochromatic kaleidoscope. Years ago, as a wedding gift, oatmeal-prune-cookie Sheila stitched me a sampler that still hangs on my wall; it reads: "Awake North Wind and Come South Wind. Then All the Trees of the Forest will Dance with Joy." Today those words mean more to me than ever before. I harvest the joy from the wind meeting the trees and I sit in it, swim in it, taking every ounce of calming pleasure I can from the knowledge that nature is beautiful and timeless. No matter what else happens to me, to my brother, to everyone I love, this singular moment is rich with winsomeness and joy.

I don't spend enough time sitting at my makeshift shrine. (Isn't that the modern meditation dilemma: stressing about relaxing?) But I am profoundly moved by the experience whenever I make it happen. The simplicity of being focused on the moment is dizzyingly blissful. And its after-effects are like rapture. Calm. Clean. Above happy. No room for improvement.

sideswiped

No TWO CANCER STORIES are the same. No one else can ever really understand what that life-threatening, body-altering, mind-skewering experience is like for another. Instant and remarkable though the kinship with a fellow survivor may be, it is only ever a partial communion. Your fear is not my fear; my children are not your children; our two paths through this confusion will never entirely twin, only intersect at certain points, run parallel at others.

Cancer is the dysfunctional lover you wish you'd never dated: you can break up, reassemble your now-stronger heart, delete his phone number, and move on to the better life you know you deserve, but you can never undo the time you spent with him. He's always going to be a part of your story. And there is always the chance you'll run into him again.

Where are the ITCs now? Right now, right this very second as you read these words, where are they? And what are they doing in my body? Are they still there, or is the withered, russet-brown skin on my left rib cage a sufficient toll paid to destroy every last one of them?

I imagine those isolated tumour cells as stealth operatives in trench coats and fedoras like a scene from *Spy vs.*

Spy—hunched over, casting a wary glance around as they advance surreptitiously, on tiptoe. They could have survived, dodged the radiation beams like seasoned Jedi deking a light sabre; perhaps one or two made a covert escape, past the radiated area altogether, and are travelling right now in search of a new home. It would only take a few to set up base camp at a remote outpost—liver? lung? ovary?—and begin to remount an attack.

Sometimes the notion of those ITCs catches me off guard, sideswiped, and skewers me with terror. Chopping vegetables, typing, running the bath for my boys—without warning, the idea of rogue cancer cells having their way with me grabs me from behind like a back-alley stalker. Then a locomotive of anxiety rolls over me like a hot, black rubber mat, flattening my spirits. I should have had my other breast removed; my god, what was I thinking? Prophylactic measures, the ultimate prevention. There could be cancer brewing in my right breast tissue, and I'd be no more aware of it than I was for all the years it brewed in my left. What was I thinking, ignoring the advice of the highly respected surgeon who recommended removing my lymph nodes? Like a burst pipe, I am instantly soaked in sweat at what I now fear was the wrong choice.

Damn it, why can't I know? Why can't someone find the nidus of deviant cell multiplication? No doctor can see any cancerous activity so small—but that doesn't mean it's not there. Why can't I swallow a liquid, a cancer-seeking iodine, that would rat out the cancer cells, turn every one of them bright neon yellow? It would highlight my body like a high school textbook at exam time, pointing out the relevant bits, finding the cancer cells and naming them. Can't somebody invent that? Why can't an ultrasound find them? A bone scan; an echocardiogram. My brain scurries through a recollection of every test I have already had, establishing baselines of tissue health before I began my treatment. But what if it's not enough? What else can we do?

The fact is there is no machine, no medicine, no herb, no technician, no healer, no possible means to track ITCs. Tiny, so tiny, they fly under all scanning radar. Isolated. Furtive scouts lying dormant until the signal—from that extra glass of wine I couldn't resist? the hair dye I'm too vain to give up?—to flutter into wakefulness and begin to multiply.

My typing fingers pause, insides trembling as I write these words, brazen siren calls to the Fates.

———

I FILL OUT THE Breast Cancer Risk Assessment form at the National Cancer Institute's website, entering the information that was true on the February day before I found a lump in my breast. Had I wondered on, say, Valentine's Day of that year whether there was any looming threat to my health, any reasonable risk that I might not be around to celebrate my love for my husband on this commemorative occasion in the future, I could have answered this questionnaire.

Age? 42

Race? Caucasian

Medical history of breast cancer, lobular or ductal carcinoma in situ? None

Age of first menstrual cycle? 10 or 11

Age of first live childbirth? 32

History of breast biopsy? None

Number of first-degree relatives (mother, sister, daughter) with breast cancer? None

Enter.

"This interactive tool was designed by scientists at the National Cancer Institute, intended for use by health professionals," I read as I wait for the calculator to compute the odds of what happened to me actually happening.

The verdict pops up on my screen. *Based on the information provided, the woman's estimated risk for developing invasive breast cancer over the next 5 years is 1% compared to a risk of 0.7% for a woman of the same age and race/ethnicity from the general U.S. population. This calculation also means that the woman's risk of NOT getting breast cancer over the next 5 years is 99%.*

I wonder if I would have wanted that information, that false reassurance. It certainly confirms what a reasonable person might have thought—that there is no logical, genetically indicated reason for a woman such as me to find a hard mass of cancerous cells lodged in her mammary tissue at this point in her relatively young life.

I retry the Risk Assessment Calculator, this time inputting my current data.

Age? 44

Race? Still Caucasian.

Medical history of breast cancer, lobular or ductal carcinoma in situ? Yes.

A window pops up on the screen, interrupting the online interview.

This tool cannot calculate breast cancer risk accurately for women with a medical history of any breast cancer.

No, I suppose no one can.

broken open

WHILE SHE MAY HAVE overstated the likelihood of any adverse health effects attributable to the emotional scars of my first heartbreak, a lot of what Nancy had to offer was true. There's no doubt that eating fields of vegetables makes us feel better; every doctor in town will support the idea of foregoing the doughnuts in favour of the raw spinach. I tried for a long time to live by the all-raw credo, following the pH Miracle diet. For breakfast I had avocado and seaweed on rye toast; for lunch I ate raw salad. My magnetic juicer worked overtime spitting out liquefied vegetables. I said no to traditional comfort foods during the time when I needed comfort most.

But eventually I began to feel beaten up by my own ambition, lacerated by the exacting requirements of such an extreme diet. It was just after an hour of Nia, the therapeutic dance class that was the latest addition to my to-do list of Healthy Approaches to Wellness, when the tightly wound mechanisms of my determination to take control of cancer began to come unsprung. Nia is a fitness routine based on the idea that movement is a pathway for self-discovery and personal transformation; it is practised in a large gym or hall, where the class is led through a sequence of cardiovascular exercises that combine jazz and modern dance with martial arts moves for a body–mind workout. Unlike the strict precision of aerobics conditioning, Nia is somewhat freestyle; dancers are encouraged to release body, mind, and soul into the exercise.

I had followed the instructor's direction well enough throughout the class, but I moved as though carrying a bookcase. My shoulders were hunched, chest clenched, a list of cancer-fighting to-do's crumpled into my brain like an accordion of corrugated cardboard. All around me, women spun and weaved their bodies with abandon, following the rhythm of the music, releasing their hearts into the dance. But not me. Knights in full armour, amputees, piano movers in mid-assignment have danced more freely than I did that day. I knew this was good for me; I followed the choreography like a robot, but I'm not sure I once felt the song. After class, stacking my purple exercise mat on top of the pile, I turned to find my dear friend Debbie standing beside me, wiping down her mat before putting it away. Her hair was wet and matted around her temples, her cheeks flushed from the vigour of her workout. "How are you feeling today?" she asked, putting her hand onto my arm.

Debbie cocks her head slightly to one side when she poses a question, as if to interrupt whatever stream of activity or thought preceded the ask, opening up her ear canals to really hear the answer.

I hesitated, fiddling with the frayed stitching at the corner of my mat. I put it down and looked up at my friend, who had brought me turmeric all those weeks ago, photographed my wretched flesh so I could know what my body had suffered whenever I was ready to see it.

Some people have eyes that take care of you just by looking your way, eyes that cannot apprehend a situation without profoundly interpreting its meaning, however oblique it may be to less nurturing glances. Debbie's eyes broke me open. I collapsed against the lopsided pile of dusty purple mats, instantly awash in tears. All the tension that had crippled my dancing was building to this. And in that moment, I gave up. Having added the stress of dietary and energetic perfection to the anxiety of MRIs, bone scans, and blood tests, the weight of responsibility for eradicating my cancer myself became too much, and I surrendered. "It's too hard, it's too much," I sobbed. "What if it's not enough? What if I can't stop the cancer growing inside me? What if this is just something over which I have no control?" The gymnasium was empty now; the last of the dancers had floated away. Deb softly rubbed my back and let my festering anxiety spill all over the floor.

The rumbling in that locked box below my good attitude had become too loud to ignore. I unloaded its contents until my face stung. I cried for the loss of a body part, the loss of my innocence, the fear of battling the dragon. I cried for the small girl who had to walk through those surgery room doors, pretending to be a brave knight. And I cried for how hard it was to surrender to not knowing, and how much harder it was to figure it all out.

Cancer doesn't care about my good attitude, my recycled toilet paper, my refillable coffee mugs, or my carpooling schedule. The promise of a perfect solution to our problems is so tantalizing—the dream of stilling a current of complications that runs through the otherwise tranquil stream of life. Our addiction to the promise keeps consumer society running at a hum.

But there are no perfect solutions. There are just moths and heartache, wrinkles in best-laid plans. Like bulky dark-coloured threads shot through fabric we keep trying to smooth.

How much do the percentages of success change with each choice we make, and what kind of math do we end up with? No matter how much exercise or energy healing I do, how many soothing restorative walks I take through the woods, how many heads of raw kale I juice, or don't ... there is no inoculation against illness. No guarantees, no way to wrestle life under control. There are merely best attempts. But surrendering the false hope that there is a single way to make everything Just So might just be the best strategy of all. Dusty grey moths will continue to flutter through my organic pantry; I'll never catch them all. They are one small part of the mystery of this whole experience; no matter the accomplishments with which we notch our belts, no matter how hard we work to understand our everyday struggles, there are some things we absolutely cannot know. And that has to be okay. In fact, if I stop—really stop—and think about it, it might even be beautiful.

Debbie held out her arm and helped me up off the ground. I wiped gymnasium floor dust off my exercise pants, and now-cold tears off my cheeks. Which is of course the wrong order for wiping; I smeared floor dust on my cheeks and wound up looking like a peasant in an amateur production of *Fiddler on the Roof.* Together, we gathered our things and walked out the door into the sunshine of the day. "C'mon," she said with a wink, "I'll buy you a green tea."

direct me aright

DRY GROUND ASSUMES MY WEIGHT: head, trunk, legs, arms evaporate into tall grasses, wind-blown. Waifish blades shimmy in and out of my sightlines, papery strands framing the canvas of blue sky. I have left the city, come to the woods for a day of peace. Away from doctors, radiation machines, shredded vegetables, prescriptions. Here, in a grassy clearing, I am on the hunt for freedom. Supine, alone, warmed by the summer sun, I come unshackled. Muscles release, thoughts slow; I notice my breath—where has it been? The warmth of the sun, a breeze waving tall grasses: these things I know, I can count on. I am safe here. To my left, the proud top of a tall pine reaches into my frame of view. Is it a white pine or Jack pine? Hard to tell from so far away. White pines have five needles, same number of needles as the letters in its name, that's how I was taught to remember. Jack pines seldom grow as straight as white pines; they look bent and irregular, like a tree with scoliosis. There are, I remember, no straight lines in nature. The creek wanders in whimsical curves, the boulder juts, the cloud shape-shifts. Even the noblest red pine in the forest veers off a straight plane, its needles taper to a pointed end. For all the right angles and smooth finishes we confine ourselves to indoors, no animal, vegetable, or mineral actually is that way. Here, in this clearing in the woods, nothing is Just So; so why does everything feel just right?

Because nature trounces aspiration. The pattern of lichen on tree bark or bare rock is perfect just the way it is; no stylist need rearrange the fallen leaves on a forest floor, no graphic designer need tweak the streaks of black ridge on white birch bark. Broadway's finest choreographers could only dream of engineering the sequence of rhythmic motion performed by every ocean wave, the effortless undulation of every song swallow flying home at dusk, the graceful sweep and bow of every windswept branch. In its crooked, unpolished disarray, there is perfect harmony in the natural world. Seed, earth, rain, sunlight, blossom, bird. The plan has been prearranged, conceived so very long ago by an invisible hand; there is no expectation of control from me. Such planning could never fit on a single list. Here in the woods, my instinct to order and manage falls silent, humbled by larger forces. Perhaps it is stilled by what Thoreau called the "subtle magnetism" of nature. "If we unconsciously yield to it," the transcendental philosopher advised, "it will direct us aright."

It strikes me what a city girl I have become: busy, accelerated, and programmed to stay on top of things, yield to almost nothing. The very notion of control seems like an urban illusion, reinforcing our detachment from the natural world. Amidst the strict details of a Martha Stewart entertaining manual, earthly snippets are integrated into the precision to stir the soul: we decorate our tables with clipping and bloom; adorn our front yards with shafts of white birch, branches of red dogwood; collect sea shells to arrange on a windowsill. An evocation of the wild in the midst of our otherwise straight-lined urban domesticity is a reminder of what we are—a connection with landscape, that which is truly timeless and outside our control. Nature is what sets us free. So why do we try so hard to tame it?

I fell in love with the outdoors as a child, felt the power and blessings of the natural world all around me every summer. As an adult, that love grew fearful; earth became my taskmaster, a demanding tycoon whose riches need protecting. I tried to control my every move, and direct those around me to do the same, in order to protect the very thing that is most uncontrollable. I must learn to live in love with nature without carrying its weight on my small shoulders.

Nature is my comfort and my passion, but cancer is part of nature too. Was my healthy lifestyle not enough? Did the stress of trying to be eco-perfect give me cancer, or is it just a gift of genetics? I try to stop asking. This disease brings enough agonies upon its victims; it should not demand a referendum on a life.

———

AFTER MY ESCAPE to the countryside, I arrive back in the city that evening. The sun has set, leaving the asphalt roads and concrete sidewalks a duo of dull greys. I pull up at the front of the house, put my hybrid car in park. The conversation on the radio has turned to Greek mythology, the story of Antaeus. I turn off the engine; the radio program continues. The speaker says that Antaeus was a formidable giant, a child of Gaia, Mother Earth. His strength derived from the earth itself and made him an unbeatable opponent in battle;

he won every wrestling match, defeated every adversary. When Antaeus challenged Hercules to wrestle, Hercules struggled against the leviathan's endless reserves of might, which swelled even further every time he was thrown to the ground. It was only when Hercules lifted him skyward and held him aloft that the giant was finally drained of his earthly powers. Being sent skyward became his undoing. Weakened in the face of the heavens, Antaeus, child of the earth, ceded his first defeat.

I turn off the radio and stare out the windshield into the darkness.

chest full of wisdom

TONIGHT, AS GRANT AND I move between the sheets in the blue-grey, pixelated, late-night bedroom light, I look down at my chest. A single orb of flesh presses up against my husband's chest, its twin felled—an abandoned goddess, carrying on alone. Beside it, the graveyard of ribs. I am snatched from the escapist pleasure of my husband's touch by the reminder of what has happened. Mourning the imperfect body I once had. I wish I still had two breasts. Sometimes the sadness surfaces like a beluga, gasping for air. How can I be grateful for being misshapen?

Looking through a pile of old photographs, the younger woman smiling back at me is healthy and strong. There is no evidence of gross bodily mismanagement, no mammoth bulges dominate the image. So why didn't I think I was beautiful and thin when these pictures were taken? Why didn't I know I was perfect just the way I was? In the spirit of gramercy, I try to appreciate my newly lopsided physique. There was, I do recall, one occasion when being single-breasted was a blessing. I'm thinking of the day I was rushing home after a shopping spree and made a gambit to dash through the subway doors just as they were beginning to close. My judgment was sufficiently addled by the bustling pace of rush hour commuters that I lunged when I really ought to have halted. My left hip, leg, and arm did make it into the train car quite comfortably. But as the sonorous thud of the heavy automatic doors landed, with significant force, directly along my middle, my right hip, leg, and arm hung loose outside, hovering above the platform, a bouquet of reusable cloth bags dangling from the crook of my elbow. Forgiveness is not a condition known to the doors (nor their operators) of most subway trains. A distinct sense of punishment is dished out to hurried, harried commuters vying for that last-second entry. You misjudged your timing, they seem to say; in future you would do well to be more punctual. As if to reinforce their point, the doors—heavy steel plates bumpered with thick shafts of stiff rubber—repeat their initial slam a few times, never actually widening long enough to release the prisoner, just reverberating the punitive squeeze. My fellow travellers were aghast at my perilous state, or so it seemed from my sandwiched perspective. Even for cynical urbanites, the inhumanity of a woman being rammed in the breast by vengeful spring-loaded doors was disconcerting. What they didn't realize, of course, is that I couldn't feel a thing. Those doors were slamming conveniently into my left breast, which is to say, the three-inch-thick wafer of silicone gel that now acts as proxy for that missing body part. The gelatinous mass of my prosthesis cushioned the force of the doors' grip, buffering my rib cage and underlying nerve endings from any discomfort whatsoever. My biggest concern was whether my purse, hanging enticingly inside the train, would get pickpocketed as I stood pinned and helpless.

———

IN A FEW YEARS, my fondling son will realize just how poor a substitute the artificial breast is for the real thing, but in the meantime, I can admit it is quite satisfactory, tucked snugly into a small piece of cotton sewn three quarters of the way around the edge of my left bra cup. I have a different prosthesis for swimming, a triangular shape that fits into the halter top of my bathing suit, a more realistic simulation of the gradation of flesh between ribs and nipple. When I exercise, though, I go *au naturel*. I have a hard enough time running long distances without a chunk of rubber shifting and bouncing across my front, and when I twist myself into yoga poses, I don't want to lose my balance distracted by a wandering breast. To spare fellow sweat soldiers at the gym any discomfort, I wear workout clothes with a built-in cup to hide the gaping nothingness on my left side. I have been single-breasted for several months now; naked imperfection is something I am getting quite used to. All in all the portable breast option works quite well—except for the ease with which I can misplace it. When a two-breasted woman forgets to pack her bra in her gym bag, she can continue her day braless and laugh about it. But when I forget my bra at home, I forget my breast at home. On more than one occasion I have had to fold my blazer over my front on an evening out, to conceal my misstep. It was after one such occasion, when I began to dress at the gym and realized I was one boob short of presentable, that I began to let myself consider the R word. Reconstruction is of course the alternative to dancing with Loretta, a second surgery to construct a replacement breast, restore flesh to the bone.

In spite of feeling queasy at the thought of further surgical intervention, I actually went so far as to book an appointment with the plastic surgeon. And here's the tantalizing reason why: radiation's permanent damage to my skin means I will not be a candidate for traditional silicone implants, but I could get a breast made out of tummy. A two-for-one deal. The promise of a flat stomach emboldened my quest for frontal balance.

When the appointment came around, the doctor had me strip from the waist up and sit hunched over on his viewing table—is there a less flattering pose for a mother of three? He then squeezed my substantial belly fat, furthering my embarrassment, and told me it was sufficient to "reinvest elsewhere." I had just enough to make one small breast, he said—all I would need. A symmetrical chest and a tummy tuck: it was like being handed two winning lottery tickets. I began to salivate. In my imagination a rebuilt chest is porn-star worthy, especially with a flattened stomach thrown into the mix. "But your new breast would be higher up than your right breast, so we'd have to raise that one afterwards. In a separate surgery, once the reconstruction has settled." My brow furrowed. "And we'd cut along your stomach muscle, so it would take a while for your core strength to return. In fact, you'd never really have your original stomach muscle back." By the time the surgeon showed me photographs of what the completed treatment would look like, my body-image fantasy bubble had long popped. For the pleasure of having two matching breasts, I'd wind up cut and scarred like the victim of a shark attack, my entire torso a jigsaw puzzle, various sections of patchwork flesh divided by intersecting slashes of mauve scar tissue.

I thanked him and his nurses for their time, and walked back down the tube-lit halls to the heavy double-door exit, and pulled it open with my right arm. My left arm still isn't strong enough for public-building doors. I remembered how much I never wanted to spend time in a hospital again, and forgot how I ever could have thought two breasts mattered.

———

NOT LONG AFTER my reconnaissance mission to the plastic surgeon, an old friend who practises massage therapy offered to give me a treatment, including a much-needed release of the chronically tight muscles and ligaments on my left chest. When I stepped out of the changing room after the session, restored and rejuvenated, she asked if she could speak her mind.

"I got a very strong intuition when I was working on the area around your scar." "Intuition?" What is it with me and outside-the-box thinkers?

"For some reason I kept picking up a sense of apology, that you felt ashamed of your missing breast and apologetic about your scar, your lopsidedness." Guilty as charged. "But I also wanted to tell you that I got the very strong sense that your left chest is full of wisdom, the kind of understanding born of experience. That part of you has a lot to teach the rest of your body."

Could this be the messenger of cancer's lesson? I begin to stare at my scar in the shower, waiting for it to speak, imparting wisdom.

For the moment, I have chosen not to airbrush over my body's history, to reinvest my surpluses to meet an arbitrary standard. Instead, every morning I dance with Loretta, to remind me of where I have been, of how perfect today will look one day in a photograph.

there is still lead in your lipstick

EARTHQUAKES, FLOODS, and hurricanes devastate more and more of the overpopulated world every year. There is still lead in your lipstick and mercury in your mascara, a dwindling bee population, and too many fossil-burning cars on the road. The evidence of our imperfect world is inescapable; I can still catalogue a tally of environmental grievances as long as a summer's day. But it no longer reads like a to-do list, with my name at the top. Today, instead of making me angry, it makes me sad. What if I get riled up for the cause, grow ever more enraged over the ongoing disasters facing the planet, stand up and speak out for what I know is right— and then get sick again?

I still live in much the way I always have—only with a lot more kale on the menu. My eco-instincts are unwavering, my values persist; I continue to tell my children to live with respect, eat more vegetables than meat, turn off the lights, and put on a sweater if they're cold. Sometimes I even stand at the podium, spreading the word. But now I come in peace. What's gone is the frantic determination to influence anyone's behaviour but my own, the conviction that I have any answers.

I want to pipe up when the nurse offers sugar cookies

at the cancer centre, lobby the school to stop wiping children's desks with chemical bleach, rally my neighbours to
rail against the smokestack emissions at the bottom of my
street ... But the indignation and fury involved in such efforts
frightens me. Embracing the moment, finding something to
be grateful for feels so much better.

But is it a cop-out?

Perhaps I'm the victim of a facile campaign to mollify
outrage, to pacify the loudmouths. When social activist and
journalist Barbara Ehrenreich went through treatment for
breast cancer herself, it disgusted her to find that relent-
less positive thinking is nothing short of adjuvant therapy
for the modern cancer patient; it's practically a prescribed
treatment. She describes an overall "cult of cheerfulness"
that she says threatens to distract us from important issues,
including how and why so many of us get cancer in the first
place. In her book *Bright-Sided: How Positive Thinking
Is Undermining America*, Ehrehreich makes the case that
positive thinking is actually fuelled by insecurity. If we really
believed that things would get better, we wouldn't need to
focus so much on positive thinking to make them be so.

I worry I've gone soft. Am I letting down the team? If I
let go of the responsibility for avoiding global catastrophe,
fail to be a round-the-clock standard-bearer, lose my place
at the front of the parade leading the troops along the Secret
Path ... my mind empties. I cannot see what that looks like.

––––––

I HAVE A DREAM.

I am inside the cottage on a warm summer day, sitting
on the floor of the living room in the familiar comfort of

the century-old log walls, under aged barnboard ceilings. A summer breeze drifts in the screen windows, carrying the voices of my three boys at play outside. I settle my bottom into a soft cushion and begin to still my thoughts into the trance of meditation. In waking life, I find meditation's blissful release somewhat elusive; many the attempt remains just that, an attempt at peace, ultimately a lost battle with my restless mind. But in my dream I am masterful, a Zen wizard of serenity. I slip wholly and immediately into a state of present contemplation. I am stillness. Tranquil and safe, I assent to all that is. I surrender my grasp on anything but this moment; *yesterday is history, tomorrow is a mystery, today is a gift*. With the grace of a sage I observe the unanimity of sensations in my body: the feel of firm hardwood supporting the pillow that holds my seat; the beads of warmth where my wrists rest gently on my bare, crossed legs; the smell of pine boughs waving outside the windows, still damp from last night's rainfall; the sound of my children squealing, teasing, splashing together at the water's edge. The erratic pulse of tiny wavelets slapping a rocky shore provides rhythmic backbeat to their cries. I am conscious of the tug at the edges of my serenity, wondering what those boys are up to, reflexively defaulting to maternal responsibility; but I resist, and hold firm to the emptiness.

Gurus of meditation speak of the mind as a tree filled with swinging, howling monkeys who need to be calmed into rest. We cannot command the monkey thoughts into silence, they caution; we must simply acknowledge them when they arise, then let them move on. I visualize a small brook, sun-dappled and burbling over smooth rocks. When the monkeys shake the tree and the mind conjures a thought or judgment, I let it flow past me along the brook, passing through the sunny spots and continuing downstream, out of sight. The babbling of the flowing water is all I can hear. And the splashing of water in the river outside the cottage walls. And the cries of my boys, their shouts, their frightened shrieks.

Why are my boys in the water without any supervision? That is the cardinal rule of life on this island: no child goes into the water without an adult on watch. We refresh that maxim at the beginning of every summer; we are emphatic about water safety. We have taken sensible, reasonable precautions to prevent the unthinkable.

I open my eyes, push up from the hard floor, and crash out the screen door. But my legs are hollow, papery shells devoid of muscle or fibre; they gyrate in cartoonish frenzy but yield little progress. I cannot reach the crest of the rocky island fast enough. The boys' cries are clearer now, shouting for help.

From the height of rock where I continue to struggle forward in agonizing slow motion, I now have a bead on the river. There is Miles, fifty feet offshore. He has swum too far out to keep up with his big brothers. His thin arms climb an invisible ladder as he bobs spastically; Reg and Harper race back toward him, eyes wild with panic. Caught up in summer's joyous spirit, they have stepped out beyond parental control, all three of them—broken the rules, together. The pull of the cool river on a hot day was too strong to resist. Flailing now, Miles's fingers grasp wildly for a hold, his wet blond head slips under the water, and is gone. Drowned while I contemplated serenity.

I wake with a guttural scream.

This must be the death rattle of the environmental crusader.

Rome is burning. *What would Gill Deacon do?*

WHAT IF, by surrendering to the imperfect beauty of what we have today, I inadvertently drop a critical thread of hope, inspiration, vision for a cleaner, healthier tomorrow? What if my children's future wellness and survival depends on me and whatever earth-saving activism I can rally right now? What if I'm making the wrong choice? Saving myself only to subject my children to a tortured future full of unpredictable weather, unsafe food, contaminated water supplies, disappearing species, and toxic chemical ingredients ubiquitous in their households? That future is already here. What will it look like when things get worse?

get back to your old life

IT'S HARD TO PICTURE the perfection peddlers working on a jigsaw puzzle. Where could they find the time? Gretchen's got closets to purge and lists of happiness to make; Gwyneth's got glutes to tone and trends to set; Martha's got topiaries to prune, wreaths to weave, rooms to tidy, miniature picture frames to paint, not to mention an empire to run, hawking directives on how to do it all, Just So. Sitting still and losing herself in a thousand-piece nature scene just wouldn't make it onto one of her lists. These domestic divas popped incongruously to mind the other day as I left an appointment with the Fairy Princess. The appointment has Day-Glo shine in my memory: wearing taupe pumps and a strand of pearls, the Fairy Princess told me I was okay. She used the words *cancer* and *gone* in the same sentence.

"Go out and live your life," she said with a smile. "You're always going to have more doctor's appointments than most of your friends, and technically it takes five years before the odds of you getting cancer drop down to match the general population, but for all intents and purposes your cancer is gone. Get back to whatever you were doing before this disease rang your bell."

Her words, ones I'd been waiting so long to hear, swirled in my head as I stood on the second floor of the cancer centre and looked down into the atrium below. At several different tables scattered throughout the waiting area, radiation patients pored over puzzles, silently communing with jigsaw Zen. Even all these weeks after I sat in among those radiation patients myself, their repose was instantly recognizable: staving the anxiety of their circumstances to focus on living in the moment, where nothing mattered more than finding the elusive snowy peak of the mountaintop, the missing piece of the sailboat's hull. I thought about what it was like to sit in that waiting room, sometimes for hours during a backlog, twenty-five times, five weeks in a row. Where better than the stark, pale landscape of a cancer hospital, surrounded by ill-health, to practise the art of acceptance? It occurred to me then that acceptance is anathema to the teachings of Martha Stewart and her many disciples: strive for more than what you have, they instruct; run one more errand to find one more object to bring life one step closer to the paragon of order.

Was that the life I should be getting back to?

I don't subscribe to Gwyneth on Goop; I don't buy Martha Stewart's books or magazines; I didn't finish *The Happiness Project*. I don't watch the television shows or download the apps that invent new ways to make our lives better. My mother, however, may be Martha's biggest customer; no surface in my parents' home is without a copy of one of her books, magazines, recipes, or design ideas. So I am no stranger to her influence. Even at a remove, I have felt the pull, the seduction of perfection. Who hasn't gazed longingly at the orderly vestibule, the pristine table setting, exquisitely lit with what appears to be eternal morning sunshine? Those images cannot but appeal to our desire for order amidst the chaos of full catastrophe living. *Make your own paint stick puppets. Get the Right look for every day. If I can't accomplish anything else today, I can do these 10 things.* As businesses, DailyCandy, the Happiness Project, Goop, Martha Stewart Inc.—they're all sure-fire successes whose brilliance is undeniable, mining the depths of a woman's desire to please, commodifying our nurturing and nesting instincts, capitalizing on the aspirational. If we only had the open space with sun pouring in the windows, and the time to make place cards out of birch bark, we'd be better mothers, partners, hosts, friends. Martha Stewart's version of Living sells the promise of control, taps into our deepest desire for order, manageability, omniscience. No doubt, the ability to control one small aspect of this oversized, tangled world provides deep comfort to a great many. It's just that it's so temporary. The thrill we feel while perusing these mastered images of Living evaporates the minute the show is over, the book is closed. Back in the dim lighting of our paint-chipped, storage-strapped disarray, we shift quickly to disappointment. Perfection porn titillates, but cannot deliver lasting fulfillment.

Gwyneth, Gretchen, Debbie, Martha. They didn't create our longing for order; they just make money off it. By presenting its promise in untold volumes, they simply reinforce an unattainable ideal. Clearly, the illusion of control was a sweet narcotic for me. I believed that I could apply the principles of order as an inoculation against suffering: Eat all the right things. Avoid all the wrong chemicals. Wash your hands neat as a pin. Keep me, my family, and our world safe from harm. It was simple math. The earth was just another thing I needed to tidy up and get right. But as the days of my fifth decade sail by at an ever-increasing pace, I notice more and more that the mess holds value. If cancer and its permanent scar are teaching me anything, it is this. What's more, the illusion of being able to avoid the mess is misleading and might just be the ultimate disservice to women. As long as it's the process we buy into, and not the result—the sewing and not the actual tablecloth—then we can harvest joy in the doing, the making, the sensory appreciation of the moment. And if we're spending the time it takes to make homemade envelopes out of wood veneer, what are we avoiding? The fear of stillness, the gulf of darkness we are afraid will consume us. But eventually, it consumes us all. As cancer horror shows go, mine was fairly humdrum. I'm still alive, with a reasonable prospect of staying that way provided I avoid electric fences during rainstorms and look both ways when I cross the street. I didn't even lose my hair (except the part I cut off in cheerful, positive-attitude preparation for the chemotherapy I didn't end up having). What I seem to have lost, though, is the ability—and the need— to get it all right, to keep up with some arbitrary, external standard of perfection. Almost dying has made me think very differently about living, and with all due respect to the grand doyenne of domestic perfection whose capitalization and branding of that word has infiltrated the consciousness of every forty-something woman on the continent, it looks less and less like the pages of a magazine with every passing day. Cancer takes so much away: employability, security, the best-laid plans, and the occasional body part. Sometimes, of course, it takes so much more. But along with the scars and the nightmares, cancer leaves something else in its trail: a stain of perspective.

Survival leaves you altered, unable to proceed quite the same way you once did. Cancer is best seen in the rear-view mirror, but its presence there has a curious impact on the journey ahead, and on the driver's ability to keep eyeballs on the road. The road I travelled before my cancer diagnosis was circuitous, splendid with much good fortune, and largely, I now realize, accidental. My career as a television personality and environmental journalist bore the optics of perfection, as Heidi was not the first to point out. A healthy family, a popular television and publishing career, and a sunshine-y take on how to save the planet, one tofu burger at a time. I believed that I had the will, stamina, and charm to defuse the cavalier disregard with which so many of us treat the earth; what's more, I believed I had the responsibility to do so, and the endless stretch of time it would take. Enter cancer, buster of personal mythologies.

burning clarity

I SOUND LIKE A STONER for saying so, but I've discovered that the sounds of children laughing and squealing in the park make a kind of music when you let them blur together. It takes a while to hear an actual melody. You must cock your head at just the right angle and hold your face up to the sun. As you discern the sensation of warmth penetrating your hamstrings from the sun-baked bench you've sat down on, the din of nearby traffic swells to a background chorus. The metallic rattle of a rusty-wheeled shopping buggy creaks by, syncopated percussion. A distant siren steals an occasional solo. There is a symphony in every moment. No narcotics required.

———

I TOOK IT AS A good sign of normalcy returning to our lives when, over a celebratory dinner marking the unofficial free pass I'd been given by the Fairy Princess, my boys began to discuss hockey—a favourite subject. The conversation turned to a tally of which teams they'd been on in the neighbourhood ball hockey league over the years and which colour jerseys they had each worn over the last couple of spring seasons.

Without exception, my recollection of each of their most recent team's name and colours were from the year before I got sick. Although I attended many of their games during the course of my treatment, I had no memory of it. I can rattle off the names of every teacher each of my kids has ever had— but have no recollection of who taught them this past year, or what their classrooms looked like. I was there, I met them all, went to most of the parent meetings and school events. Just as I was present for annual birthday parties and Mother's Day celebrations. There is much I could recount about previous years' family gatherings and celebrations, but during that year of cancer, the picture is black. Details of life's passing carnival never registered. My mind was elsewhere.

Looking back now, that period has become a strip of time that didn't exist, except in the hospital or in relation to cancer.

Stress narrows focus, as it must. When we put our heads down and grit our teeth to get through a challenge, the brain cannot absorb extraneous information that is not directly related to survival. Bob Fowler, the Canadian diplomat kidnapped by al Qaeda for four months, told me he had the same experience during his harrowing tenure in the African desert. He was in town visiting his daughter—a good friend of mine—and her family for Christmas, exactly one year after he originally went missing. I commented that it seemed like only days ago that he had been coming for last Christmas, a plan that had been sabotaged by the kidnapping. While others around us appeared surprised that such difficult years for both of us should have seemed to pass quickly, Bob agreed he knew just what I meant. "It feels now like those months flew by, but it sure didn't feel like it then."

During crisis, time is both interminable to experience in the moment and yet barely exists in retrospect. Looking back on the hardship that has been endured, and survived, time is compressed, flattened into a dehydrated version of events. Bob and I both felt the same stenosis of memory, a collapsing of every other detail in the world around us that colours normal life, marks the passage of our regular days. Stress, fear, and focus on a single outcome strip away every other tidbit of recollection; shreds of extraneous information cease to matter. Crisis affords burning clarity. About what holds value and what does not.

———

I RETURN TO MY DESK, to the bustle of work, and to the endless patter of communication. Today I turn away from my desk and take a moment to gaze out the window of my home office. Starlings dance along the wires that criss-cross the alleyway behind my house. The rooftops of neighbouring garages slant at mismatched angles, as though arranged by Georges Braque. The entire assortment of back-alley architecture has a Cubist irregularity to it, sublime in its own pedestrian, urban way. My eyes scan the view for movement in the trees, looking for a salutation from the wind.

The tea I drink is green—loaded with antioxidants—and hot; sometimes I notice how it feels cascading down my left side, behind Loretta. Perhaps tomorrow, if I'm feeling daring, I'll relish the forbidden pleasures of an oatmeal chocolate chip cookie. Or two. I'm hoping all those antioxidants in my tea will cancel out the sugar. But I can't know for sure.

why am i still here?

MY NEIGHBOUR MADELEINE baked bread for my children when I was sick. She brought over three small loaves, still warm; each boy claimed one for himself. They smeared fresh butter on the crumbling slices, gobbled them like Dickensian ruffians. The loaves were gone in mere minutes, a pre-dinner indulgence I would not normally allow. The kindness of a thoughtful friend can override a great deal, including best-laid plans.

Madeleine is a superb cook, a foodie. Over the years since she moved in, my boys have rung her bell occasionally, offering to shovel her walk, or hoping to sell her a raffle ticket; invariably, she greets them with a smile of delight and a plate full of fresh baking. "You're my recipe testers, guys," she tells them. "What do you think?"

They mutter polite appreciation, mouths bursting with raspberry scones, chocolate chip cookies made with kamut flour, other delicious experiments. They are dumbfounded at their good fortune; that the monotony of door-to-door soliciting might actually lead into a baker's kitchen, complete with free samples. Madeleine's eyes sparkle. She smiles and tells them these delicious treats are actually a failed batch; they'd better take the rest of them home.

One time I left a small box of kumquats on her doorstep, bright orange bullets. I had mentioned to her that I had no idea what to do with them, but had been lured into buying them by their charming shape and colour. Madeleine turned them into delicious kumquat marmalade. I don't know her well, but she has brought several memorable moments of pure joy to my sweet boys, reached my family's heart through our collective belly.

In the middle of a workday at my desk not long ago, I opened an email that made me wince: Madeleine's husband, Don, had pancreatic cancer, it said, and would likely not survive the summer.

He is a handsome, quiet man in his early fifties, often out tending the garden when I pass. I would not claim to know him; still I was stunned by the news of his illness.

It always hits like a brick in the face. No matter how many times it happens, the news of a cancer diagnosis strikes like a well-aimed kick. I closed my laptop and wept.

Why? Why him? Why now?

In his "biography" of cancer, *The Emperor of All Maladies*, Dr. Siddhartha Mukherjee describes the culture of the disease; Cancer World, he calls it. Every minute following diagnosis takes place in a parallel universe, on Planet Cancer. We become defined by the diagnosis. Mukherjee writes of patients who feel that, even when they are not in the hospital, they are in the hospital. We talk of The C Word, fearful to name the beast lest it strike. More than any other disease, he writes, cancer wields the power to intimidate, terrorize, dominate the conversation.

But here's what else I notice: no matter how successfully we steer the rocket ship home from Planet Cancer, we can be transported back in an instant. Where others may stargaze in peace, we who have spent time in its peculiar orbit will always notice Planet Cancer in the night sky. And we watch, trembling on the inside, as countless ships launch around us, bound for the same place we've been; we keep inventory of those whose flights return and those whose do not.

Don did not survive the summer. Another fallen soldier: a loving, decent parent and husband, a friend, a colleague, a gardener.

Even as we take bold, forceful strides away from cancer's experience, toward a future of health and harmony, it has the potency to draw us back with a snap, like a destructive ex-lover who knows all our weaknesses. We know he's no good for us, yet one sideways look can lure us to return for more torment.

The emotional undertow begins. Guilt (I survived!) immediately followed by fear (For now...). Perhaps I need to earn the right to stay. Am I doing enough?

Why am I still here?

Not that I'm complaining, but why me? Paul Quarrington has died. Lynn Redgrave has died. My uncle has died. The father of Madeleine's children has died. Famous or anonymous, hundreds of thousands of people died of cancer the same year I was sick.

But I got better.

Does that mean something? Is there a purpose I am meant to serve? How are survivors meant to interpret the random logic of who goes and who gets to stay? Is there a message, an inscrutable pattern to be deciphered from the statistics, some sort of ancient code to be read like tea leaves? I felt so certain of my purpose as a self-appointed planet-fixer; now that calling is much less clear. What is cancer's message? And how will I know if I've heard it?

I float along with the hum on a crowded sidewalk, catch myself feeling blessed to be here, back in functioning form, able to blend in again with the rest of society, no longer defined by my disease. But then confusion interrupts the appreciation. As I pass a fast-food joint, unhealthy-looking strangers shuffle in and out, the reek of cheap saturated fats clinging to their clothing. Why don't they have cancer? Why Don and not them? Why me? Is their number to come up next? Do I even wish for it to be so, just so that there will be some logic to this disease, a pattern in the chaos?

Wash your hands neat as a pin, circus clowns are marching in. For all the years that I needed a boost at the sink to wash up before dinner, that was the message written (likely in lead-based paint) on the stool in the bathroom, a cheery credo of cleanliness. It was just one aspect of the preparedness-for-wellness training I received at my mother's knee. I learned that there are ways to protect yourself, to mitigate pain and suffering. Eat well, sleep well, and you'll be well. Which is, of course, true ... up to a point.

We look for answers and explanations when people get cancer, evidence that they somehow chose the path that led them to cancer's door. So-and-so died of lung cancer? Oh, well, he smoked—code for: He Asked For It. Our compulsive need to find reasons for the deaths of others, to make excuses for them happening, is born out of our deeply held discomfort with the inevitability of our own death. With the possible exception of Zen monks, fear of death is universal. So we claw and grasp for understanding when it happens

around us, ascribing pattern and logic to ultimately unknowable circumstances.

In the same way, those of us who evade death's grasp—for
now—attempt to find rational explanations as to why. It is
tempting to think that my positive outlook made me better.
But does that mean that my neighbour's husband and the
rest of cancer's victims just didn't try hard enough? Surely
not. In the locker rooms on both sides of the stadium, each
team practises positive thinking before the big game. Both
sides go into the championship final visualizing victory,
but only one team will win. Did the winners do a better job
harnessing the law of attraction? Or are they just the team
that scored the most points? As the Danny Michel song goes,
"If God's on your side, then who's on mine?"

How do we behave as survivors, doing the Chancy
Dance? We sport a face of optimism, a daily costume donned
to muffle the pulsing beat of fear and wonder. Our joyful
vigour is fuelled by having successfully battled the beast;
the cancer survivor is what Alice Trillin, in her 1981 essay
"Of Dragons and Garden Peas," likens to the knight who has
slain a dragon. While he may feel and act like a conquering
hero, only the most foolish and cocky of knights would ever
relax on the job, knowing that dragons "are never quite dead,
and might at anytime be aroused, ready for another fight."

What if those trilliums were just trilliums?

There was a novelty factor to being a cancer patient,
adding a perverse thrill to the exercise—a gauntlet was laid,
I struggled to meet the challenge, pass the test. Experiencing
the agonies of labour and childbirth for the first time, there
is an aspect of that novelty that makes the ordeal curiously
manageable, one part of the mind seated to the side watching

the body's performance with wide-eyed fascination. But the second labour is stripped of that charm; the insult of familiarity compounds the pain. The discouragement of knowing what comes next can easily trump chutzpah.

Would I be able to rally that much grace and composure again were the dragon to reappear for a second battle? Will I be ashamed of that positive attitude if it turns out not to have done the job completely? Every word I write on these pages will reek of crow if my survivorship proves to be temporary.

When I think about what it would be like to battle cancer again, without the first-timer's wide-eyed observation, I feel my insides collapse. My bravery is gone at the very thought, a popsicle-stick castle in a cyclone.

————

IN HIS BOOK *Death, Grief, and Mourning*, Geoffrey Gorer wrote about how we deal with grieving and loss in modern North American society. He observed that we tend to consider the deflated energy of mourning and loss "as morbid self-indulgence, and to give social admiration to the bereaved who hid their grief so fully that no one would guess anything had happened."

For whom, then, the cancer patient's positive attitude? Was it for my benefit, or to mitigate the consideration of their own mortality for those around me?

It occurs to me that writing this book is my silent, daily communion with the deflation of defeat, loss, and grief, a revisiting of the sadness, the confusion. In public, that is largely shelved. Until word comes that another soldier has fallen. Then, as do we all, I feel reminded of how close it is, of how little I understand.

tending

WITH MY LEFT HAND I reach for a glass on a high shelf, straining on tiptoes. I feel the twinge of severed muscle and tendon along my left side, but otherwise function with complete range of motion; I marvel at how much mobility has returned. My lymphatic system is intact, labouring silently to bolster my immunity. The gamma rays have drained from enough of my organs to return my energy and sleep patterns to normal. I can even hold my downward dog; my flimsy arms are getting stronger. The colour of my once vinaceous scar has faded through the full spectrum of mauves to what is now a dull white.

My body, what's left of it, is back in business. I was the patient; now I am the survivor.

Yesterday, just over a year since Lisa retired as commanding officer of my meal brigade, I accompanied her on the ninety-minute drive to spend the afternoon with her dying mother. Her efforts on my behalf through my own medical ordeal never crossed my mind when she asked for the company. I simply rose, as many of her friends have, to the call for help from a friend in need. In spite of living so far away, as an only child Lisa bears the sole burden of responsibility for her widowed mother in these final days of her life.

As good friends do, we talked and laughed most of the way, in spite of the sad purpose for our journey. We did not speak of how much Lisa had done for my family, how much care she had marshalled to ease our troubles through much of the previous calendar year. Those days seemed far behind us now. Lisa turned on the wipers as bleak November rain began to fall, lightly at first, then occasionally in hard torrents, making it hard to see the road ahead. A pine needle lodged underneath one wiper blade left a pesky trail of smeared water trailing back and forth across the other-wise smooth, clear windshield. We passed a grey barn on the side of the road, boards so weathered and dilapidated they curved and swelled like waves, as though the barn was made of fabric. A building whose time had come.

At the hospital, I watched as Lisa negotiated with the pretty, young palliative care nurse over how many cc's of morphine were appropriate, advocating for her near-voiceless mother, and as she held up her mother's weak, limp body to rearrange the pillows for comfort. Tending as she had been tended to.

On the ride home in the dark, Lisa told me how deeply relieved she was that I had been there with her, not just for the company on the long rainy drives, but as a witness to the frightening confusion of watching your mother slip away from life. A second set of eyes and ears to make sense of medical information, to distill the painful reality of imminent death. She was so glad to be able to drape the blanket of burden over an extra set of shoulders. Climbing in the company of a friend, this particular hill seemed less steep.

I told her I knew what she meant.

Soon I'm sure that I will sign up for someone else's meal duty, run someone else's errands, bring someone else distracting cheer when, as the numbers insist that they must, another friend will walk this shadowy path through cancer. With luck, my footprints will have been somewhat helpful in marking the trail. Life after forty seems to be a series of shifts from acolyte to basket case and back again. One day we hobble, the next we carry someone else on our backs.

should is overrated

L ATELY MY DAYS are about as serene as the running of the bulls in Pamplona. I am late for meetings, strapped for cash, peppered with more grey hairs every time I look. My mobile phone pings and beeps like a pinball machine, executing my daily reminders, jostling me from one commitment to the next, one side of town to the other. I sit in traffic in a heat wave, sweating profusely, agitated that I'm now late for the mammogram that will examine my one remaining breast for any sign of cancer. I'm terrified to repeat this procedure, my first since my diagnosis; every hallway, technician, gown, and examination table is a wretched reminder of where I spent too many months.

I try to get my mother off an ill-timed suppertime phone call without hurting her feelings, race to get dinner made with what little we have in the fridge, before my three boys strike a mortal blow in a fit of hunger-induced fisticuffs. One brother inadvertently whacks another in the face with the butt of a hockey stick, but of course the injured party considers the blow intentional. I hang up from one generation, try to broker peace among the members of another. Dinner burns in the process.

My life is not special in its chaos. But now I am able to summon that burning clarity. In the midst of the mental whack-a-mole match that is getting through the rumpus of life, I stop. I try to find what to be grateful for in the situation, which usually involves gazing at the nearest tree branch and noticing how it moves in the wind. I breathe deeply, even just for a minute. Rather than try to master one accomplishment and scurry past it on to the next mission, I simply notice the moment as it is going by and feel grateful to be here to witness it. And I check to make sure that what I'm doing is a Want, not a Should. Should is overrated. Should puts someone else in the driver's seat, like celebrity divas of domestic perfection. Should has been deeply programmed into our vocabulary; it clings like a resistant virus.

Socrates cautioned, "Beware the barrenness of a busy life." I would argue that not all lives lived in a busy haze are barren, only the ones in which the busy-ness is fuelled by obligation rather than pleasure.

I still catch myself composing tweets in my mind during Savasana pose, or otherwise frittering away moments of gratitude. A litany of to-do's creeps back into my psyche like a pulled thread, easily caught; it gathers the rumpled fabric of my shoulders and draws them tighter around my neck. Cancer's burning clarity is not a permanent effect—which doesn't seem fair, really. You'd think immutable serenity would have been a decent trade for a valuable body part. But I'm not going to turn peace of mind into a task on my to-do list—stressing about relaxing. It's not always easy to muster grace. But if we really boil it down, there is always something to be grateful for.

Cancer made me scared that I would die and miss all

the fighting and hugging and talking and peacemaking and knee scraping and storytelling and lesson learning of life with my beloved boys and husband. Cancer made me scared that I would lose both my breasts, so the stress of getting to an appointment to have the remaining one examined, in its own weird way, is itself a blessing. I am grateful to be able to drive a car on my own, walk in the door of the hospital a healthy woman, and shove one breast into the panini press for a mammogram. Looking down at the sketch on the mammogram technician's standard worksheet, I see the giant cursive lowercase W, two swoopy half-circles with a dot in the centre; a child's rough sketch of two boobs. On the sheet dedicated to my test, one of the swoops has an X through it, my other breast deleted with the stroke of a pen, denying whatever used to be.

Bloody lucky, I am, to be here for all of it.

———

A FRIEND IS IN TOWN from Los Angeles, where she is a successful film producer. We talk over drinks one night, after months of not seeing each other. She is disillusioned, says the movie business doesn't deserve all the glamour of the Hollywood image. She wants to be sure she is doing something else in ten years.

"Do you ever think about what you'll be doing with your career in ten years?" she asks. "I mean do you have a plan, or goals for where you want to be? I know that's the sort of thing we think of doing when we're in our twenties or thirties, making ten-year goals, but I still do it, you know? I don't have an exact plan for where to get to in the next decade, but I know I don't want to be doing this anymore. Do you?"

She fingers an olive from the antipasto platter we've both been picking at on the table. She pops it in her mouth, looking at me for an answer.

"I don't even know if I'll be alive in ten years," I tell her, with as little melodrama as possible. I want to avoid any cloying survivor-speak, god forbid. But I just don't find myself worrying about the ten-year plan right now. "I'm really happy to be healthy and I'm trying to make sure that the choices I make each day, including what I do for work, are choices that keep me happy and healthy. Fuck, I must sound like some phony wise cancer saint," I laugh and make a face. "But that's all I can manage right now."

My friend is quiet for a moment. She looks down at the floor as she reaches a hand up to her mouth to remove the olive pit, placing it on a small plate littered with cheese rinds and crusts of bread, hardening in the dry restaurant air.

———

LIVING WITH GRATITUDE and extracting every ounce of joy and satisfaction in any given day is a way to extend the time that we have. Not planning for tomorrow, making lists of things to do. Be a human being, not a human doing. It's hard to maintain that focus now that I am well. I feel the preying gluttons of stress, juggling, planning, organizing, and perfection all creeping closer around me, tugging me back to the frantic pre-cancer pace of my modern urban life. Here comes the reflex to seek perfection, creeping back as an accompaniment to wellness. Is it possible to ever truly live in the moment and abandon our wiring without being in a state of perilous health?

But now, with a little effort, I can still the avaricious control monkeys in an instant—if only for an instant. There's a place of gratitude in each moment that is calm, rich with relief. The tangled confusion of Miles's bright yellow hair frizzing in every direction when he wakes up. The pattern of holes in the snow over a sewer grate. The wagging slap of the dog's tail at the first sign of movement toward the front door. There they are, like warm tea to slake the thirst and chill of a heartsick wanderer.

the scale of power

O N **WHAT MUST HAVE BEEN** the hottest day of the summer, my boys and I were cooling ourselves in the river at my parents' cottage. Reg and Harper showed off their strong strokes, racing to the nearby raft. Miles and I held hands as we jumped off the end of the dock; he likes to see if we can hang on to our grip even when we land underwater. Climbing up the ladder after a jump he turned to me, dripping, and said, "Remember last summer when you couldn't come to the river, Mama?" So matter-of-fact, as though recalling a movie we had seen together.

I told him how oppressive and unbearable the heat had been in the city during my weeks of treatment the previous year, how I had missed the water, the birds, the pine trees.

My once-terrifying cancer battle had become a story we told in our family, a hurdle the boys now took in stride. A challenge we had survived together.

Just then I noticed a dash of lightning slice the sky in the distance. "Out of the water, boys!" I hollered. "Storm's coming!"

We grabbed our towels and hurried off the dock, up the slope of rock toward the cottage. As we scrambled up the incline I saw the light make a shift; the rock, the blueberry bushes, the stately pines took on the matte finish that precedes every storm on the river. And then, as I knew it would, the heat vanished as the temperature took a sharp turn. When we reached the crest of the rocky slope I turned around to face the coming storm. "Stand here, boys, just for a minute or two," I called, over the growing wind. "Let's watch it coming." As my mother had done with Jake and me so many times, I wrapped my arms around their bare, bony shoulders and we stood firm together in our wet bathing suits, braced against the gale. "The rain looks like a white curtain!" Harper shouted, his summer-blond hair plastered to his forehead. "I can't see Fraser Island anymore!" The Laurentian foothills flanking the opposite shores had become invisible, and the neighbouring islands disappeared one by one behind a sheet of driving rain advancing across the now-black river. Inside, my mother and father would be pulling furniture away from the screened windows on the veranda to keep it from getting soaked by the wind-driven rains. She would be getting nervous, seeing her only grandchildren facing down the business end of a Three-Day Blow. Outside the skies darkened. Raindrops began to nip at our skin as Reggie, Harper, Miles, and I stood huddled in our damp towels near the stately pine, amazed that we had felt so limp with humid heat only moments ago. I waited for the delicious point when the army of raindrops would land on our shore and march straight at us and our squeals would be lost in the howl of wind as we skittered inside to watch, gasping and laughing and dripping under the protective roof of the old log cabin. But the moment never came. Suddenly, the storm was too much; nature wasn't playing the same game anymore. The winds overtook us, stronger than we could ever pretend to resist. The heavy wooden chairs my parents liked to sit in every evening to watch the sun setting over the river now tumbled past us, tossed across the rock like a handful of jacks. The sheet of white rain lost its charm as it careened into a horizontal blade and pelted us from the side. Boys and mother shrieked and wailed as the magic of storm watching crashed among the three-foot waves spraying the island's rocky shore. The scale of power tipped and we were punished for having presumed we might own it, describe it, enjoy its titillation. As we ran toward shelter, Miles's feathery weight was steered more by the wind's might than his own and he began to cry. Reggie grabbed his arm to hold him on course. Laces of wet hair slapped into our eyes, beach towels were ripped from our grasp and flapped like colourful toy flags. I heard a ripping sound like a giant's arm rent from its socket, then the anguished roar of a thousand mourners wailing in unison: a million tiny roots that had nourished a sixty-foot pine tree on nothing but Canadian Shield rock for the last hundred years, and withstood the battering of countless storms before this one, finally gave up and let go. The boys reached the cottage ahead of me and flung open the screen door. Stumbling to catch up to them I turned to see the glorious pine that had sheltered us for so many generations crash to the ground beside me. Its branches plastered across the window screens and doorway, muddling my entrance. My mother stood inside the door, tears streaming down her face as she watched the majestic familiarity of her favourite land-scape wrenched out of place.

Miles began to wail the word on all of our lips, "Noooooooooooooo!"

Mother Nature holds all the cards.

a definite endpoint

In 1993, RESEARCHERS at Harvard Medical School's Department of Behavioural Medicine and the State University of New York's Department of Psychiatry conducted a comparative study into the psychological impact of infertility as compared with a variety of other traumatic health conditions. The study, published in the *Journal of Psychosomatic Obstetrics and Gynecology*, tracked women suffering from infertility and compared them to women of similar age dealing with either chronic pain, hypertension, HIV, cardiac-rehabilitation, or cancer. While some groups scored higher or lower on depression or anxiety, the global symptom scores for the infertile women were equivalent to those of the cancer patients. For either diagnosis, it was noted, the average patient experiences the future in stark terms, either black or white. For cancer patients the outcome is death versus cure, and for infertility patients, sterility versus biological parenthood. The researchers concluded, "Cancer and infertility treatments are comparable in that there is a definite endpoint, a single, objective criterion of success for the treatment: cure and a live birth, respectively."

———

WARM AUGUST AIR blows through the cooling vents in my car on this early morning drive to my brother's house—air conditioning must be broken. I make a mental note to have it repaired. The windshield is peppered with stringy seed pods fallen from a tree on my street—thwarted fertility, its annual yearning to reproduce itself interrupted by metal and glass; the car getting in nature's way, not for the first time. The urban tree lives out a single life, casting no legacy into the future by sowing seeds onto streets and cars. My heart beats faster as I pull up to their door, though I feel a familiar calm. Gratitude for this moment surges through me. Incongruously, as I search for my brother's house key on my chain, a photograph pops into my head. Shot the morning of my mastectomy surgery, it is a self-portrait taken in front of the hospital doors. Dark glasses reflect the day's sunshine, masking what must have been sadness in my eyes; but the rest of my face beams confidence. It carries the promise of the trilliums: Everything will be all right—or so I told myself. Inside, I gently close my brother's front door. The house is quiet, the air sluggish with the pastiness of lost sleep. Jake comes slowly down the stairs, carrying his small son. In time, he will become more practised at descending stairs holding such precious cargo, but on this, his second morning as a father, he proceeds with caution. He hands me the baby, the one who mirrors his likeness, the one I have driven home from summer vacation on the river to hold; the one we have all waited so long to meet. He is Foster, after our great-grandmother's family name. And his loveliness is beyond compare. It does not occur to me to fear for the kind of world this child will inherit, to worry about the quality of his drinking water or the rate of overpopulation and unstable weather he will contend with as an adult. In part, I suppose, because he is not my own offspring. But even more so, because he has brought so much joy, right now, to so many people I love. As he grows older, I will feed him locally grown vegetables and rub his belly with safe, natural oils. I will read him *The Lorax* and tickle his little piggy toes. I will show him how to tell the difference between a Jack and a white pine. Perhaps we will watch a summer storm together. But for now, I take Foster outside to settle his fragile cries (isn't this the role every auntie loves to play?). Rocking and swaying under the canopy of maple on my brother's quiet street, I gaze down at the round, gorgeous pink flesh that is his head, parked at my left chest. Where my breast once was. He squirms in his flannel wrap, tiny slatted eyes crinkled in consternation. I mutter a rusty hodgepodge of shushes and lullabies, hauled up from a recess of memory. Eventually, it becomes clear this tiny boy is hungry. His head begins to turn toward me, rooting at my prosthesis. Oh, my good man, don't waste your reaching on that slab of gelatinous plastic; I've got nothing in there for you. Nothing but a beating heart. I turn back to the house to return him to his mother, smiling as I look up from my left chest to the branches swaying gently in the faint August breeze. I cannot help but be struck by the trade-off, and it occurs to me to wonder if everybody got what they needed.

wrapped in barbed wire

LUCIANO IS A QUIET ITALIAN gentleman who lives around the corner. He is small, no bigger than my twelve-year-old, and simply dressed—an urban peasant. Occasionally my family and I see him driving around the neighbourhood in his rattly old Subaru, his capped head barely visible above the steering wheel, his sightline grazing just above the dashboard. But mostly we see him walking with his wife—shuffling, really—up and down the alley that connects our two houses.

The first time I met Luciano he was standing in the alley beside my neighbour's high wooden fence. A pear tree grows just inside the fence; several of its branches overhang the alley. Luciano was holding a pole, longer and thicker than a broomstick; at the end of the pole was an open-ended tin can, attached to the pole with kitchen string. A taller man might have been able to pinch a few low-hanging pears from the neighbour's tree with a simpler contraption, or perhaps none at all. But in his seventy-something years of being vertically challenged, Luciano had learned to be resourceful when it comes to reaching things. Hoisting the pole straight up above him, he cupped the open tin around a pear, then twisted the pole. Lowering it down, he gleefully retrieved the fruit, handed it to his wife to load into her apron, then began the pilfering process anew. I came across the two of them midway through this act of petty crime. I was new in the neighbourhood and didn't yet know pear-harvesting protocol. Was this a long-standing tradition? Sure, Luciano, take as many as you want, we can't eat them all anyway. Or was this unassuming little retiree simply sharing the community's resources the way he had in the old country?

No one ever mentioned it, and I soon forgot to concern myself with the appropriateness of the deed. What I never forgot was the youthful playfulness shared between Luciano and his apron-clad partner in crime. They smiled at one another with joy over the newly picked pears; she hollered what I took to be encouragement at him in delighted Italian. They formed a well-oiled machine, a smooth operation with years of practice at completing tasks in tandem. Every evening they walked together, Luciano on the left, his hands clasped behind him, his capped head slightly downturned. His wife was always one step behind on the right, looking around at what this day had wrought on the familiar land-scape of their community.

A few weeks after my radiation treatment had ended, as I muddled through the requisite what-just-happened-to-me confusion, I ran into Luciano. I had not seen him in months, except possibly out my window.

"Howa' you doing?" he asked. We didn't usually exchange more than a cursory hello, a friendly acknowledgment of the day's weather or my children's insatiable appetite for street hockey, so I was surprised at the personal question. "Oh, I'm doing really well, thank you," I replied. Did he know I'd been sick? Surely he wasn't just asking out of the blue, but I didn't want to open up that can of worms with someone I hardly knew, unless I could figure out how to discuss oncology in Italian.

"They tolda' me you sick." He pointed at the house with the pear tree in the backyard.

"My wife, she wasa' very sick too. She no here a'no more. She gone."

I thought of the apron, cradling pears.

"Oh, Luciano, I'm so sorry," I said. "When did that happen?"

"Two weeks. Very sad."

He stopped, unable to continue.

There it was, right here beside me. Unspeakable loss; the well-oiled machine put in park and permanently dismantled.

Luciano nodded gratefully as I sputtered heartfelt apologies, then he shuffled to his left and began to walk away, continuing his routine as best he could. Hands clasped behind his back, he plodded on, his capped head hung.

There is so much loss in a given day. Aching hearts are all around us, yet the swirling roar of a full life often mutes their cry. Wellness can muffle life's details. It offers no reason to question. But illness recalibrates the senses to suffering and defeat.

————

IN THE BATTLE FOR LIFE, a frontier is crossed. Light fades, hope recedes, storm clouds roar into view. The soldier stands alone. There are others—commanders, generals, centurions—but their words are hard to hear in the cacophony of assault; their artillery cannot be counted on. Called to wage war against a dark stranger, the soldier steps forward, into new territory. A salvo of pain erupts in a monsoon of fear and threat. The soldier is lost, facing unknowable challenge.

Something happens out there on the battlefield. Perhaps it is a gradual light appearing on the horizon; it might be a smattering of melody that sneaks into the soldier's heart. In whatever form, grace most certainly presents itself—a trusted companion, who has covered this uneven ground many times before. As the sky begins to brighten, the soldier locates courage, then determination. And at some point, in the ever-growing dawn, the soldier observes the surrounding battalion as if for the first time and hears the songs they sing as they march.

———

IN MANY WAYS my life is back to the way it used to be. Keys go missing, children throw fits over homework, pants are too tight, dogs vomit on new furniture, bills pile up, life trundles on. But there has been a shift. Now every moment, from calamity to delight, is passed through a filter I carry with me. When I try to describe it, I envision Frodo's precious ring. Huge, more like a shimmering lifebuoy, it sits in my gut, weightless, radiating clarity. It is the gift of cancer. Someone once told me cancer is a gift, but it comes wrapped in barbed wire. You have to go through a lot of pain and excruciating effort to unwrap it before it can reveal its value. But once it has been opened, it is unparalleled treasure.

What is the ring made of? Knowledge of what we have, appreciation of its brevity; acceptance of the shortcomings, erasure of petty vanities; awareness of the impermanence of every single one of us; the observation of loss; and ultimately, peace.

I could not have known this repose, this lightness born of unthinkable fear, without the jolt of perspective that a campaign against cancer provides. When you are swollen to bursting with your forthcoming first child and parents tell you (as they love to do, misery's predilection for company being what it is) that you are about to experience exhaustion of a magnitude previously unimaginable, you think you know what they mean. Or when they tell you (joy's propensity for contagion being what it is) that none of the fatigue will matter because you will love this swaddled creature in a way you had never conceived possible, you test the stretches of your imagination and feel sure that once again, you are prepared; you think you know what they mean.

But then the baby comes. With the breaking of waters comes an opening of emotional floodgates, ushering you into a new paradigm altogether. Your entire system shifts, discovers a new gear that wasn't even shift-into-able before. You enter an unfamiliar orbit that is different, yet strangely familiar; comfortable, like knowledge from a past life. "Ohhh," you think to yourself one night at a previously unthinkable yet now routine pre-dawn hour of bleary-eyed wakefulness, nodding your head slowly as we do when fathomless realization takes hold. "Now I know what they meant." And you smile to yourself at how little you understood before, even when you thought you did. Because how could you know until you knew?

To be well again after being sick is to walk with one foot always on the edge of the cliff, one eye ever casting a sideways glance at the abyss.

For me, the gift wrapped in barbed wire is a chuckle. Not an outright guffaw, not a gesture of judgment or self-satisfaction. Just a few sharp exhalations from an upturned mouth, revelling in all that we have. I chuckle at myself for attempting control; I chuckle at how spectacularly interesting the world is. And I chuckle at my marvellous good fortune to be here taking part.

If I tell you the things that swell my heart and still my worry, they may ring hollow, or worse, saccharin. The crisp pattern of sunlight and shadow on the snow-covered rooftops out my window; the giggly chorus of girlfriends gathered over wine; the rhythmic trance of chopping and assembling ingredients to feed my loved ones; the envelope of silence surrounding me on a walk through a cathedral of pine forest; the engine of determination propelling children's legs as they run their hardest toward the finish line; the faint chuffs of Foster's delicate breath as he wiggles in my arms. That is part of my list; yours, Dear Reader, may be quite different. There is no prescription for finding moments of gratitude in every day; there is simply the choice.

Appreciate every day because it may be your last. You can't control which way the river bends. There is no such thing as perfect. Don't worry, be happy. The hackneyed wisdom adorning bumper stickers and coffee mugs grows legs, tentacles into meaning. Then the comfort behind the cliché flows like honey in the bloodstream.

Is a cancer survivor automatically wiser? Of course not. Do we all make better decisions? I wish. But at the end of a long day of full-catastrophe living, a glowing ring gleams in the gut. Perhaps it is nothing more than a compensation we administer to ourselves to mollify the frustration of drawing the cancer card; perhaps it is self-soothing, comfort for the ongoing sadness of having suffered. I don't know where it comes from; I only hope it lasts.

acknowledgments

I have much to be grateful for, enough to fill another book. But for our purpose here, my appreciation can be distilled to two blessings: strength and encouragement.

Strength: the ability to keep going. I am strong and alive and healthy enough to write because of the exceptional care of several sparkling gems of the medical community. So, many thanks to Dr. David McCready for his prompt and exacting attention; to Dr. Rebecca Dent for her warmth and smarts; to Anne Blair for making the cancer centre feel almost homey; to Dr. Eileen Racovitch for her kindness and bullet-proof good judgment; and to Dr. Glykeria Martou for her exquisite skill at making me feel whole again.

The non-professionals who gave me strength are my El Cancero posse of dear friends and relations. There are some things in life we truly never forget. Thank you for all you did to get me and my boys through.

To my beloved family, including its newest member, Pippa, thanks for buoyancy amid choppy waters.

And to the four men I live with who endured a very female ordeal, thank you for unwavering love and honesty.

Encouragement: the stimulus to try, to believe, and to dare to fail. That has to be the greatest gift one human being can give another—especially when that other is a writer. This collection of musings owes its existence as a book to the encouragement of so many people.

To Esta Spalding, who gave me the courage to try a different kind of writing.

To Ashley Bristowe, cheerleader for notetaking during treatment and for my application to the Banff Centre.

To Ian Brown, Katherine Ashenburg, and Don Gillmor, my clever and caring editors at the Banff Literary Journalism program. Thank you for your patience, for inspiring me to become a better writer, and for teaching me how to make art out of memory.

To Cathy (Marie) Buchanan, for using expletives in the most complimentary fashion upon reading my first draft. You believed this should be a book, and you helped me see how to get it there. Thanks too for glorious and productive time at your writers' retreat cottage, where the bowl of fresh limes is always full.

To Emmy Laybourne, for bolstering along the way. Thank you for such thoughtful, careful reading of my manuscript, enough to make your mascara run. You make me happy to be a writer.

To Emma Waverman, for such good company on the bumpy road to a completed manuscript.

To Andrea Magyar at Penguin Canada, for all those exclamation marks upon reading the manuscript. As always, you and your terrific Penguin team made the completion of this book a pleasure.

To Samantha Haywood, the best agent a gal could ever hope for. Thank you for your faith and for always having my back.

And to Grant Gordon, who belongs on both lists. You give me strength every day, more than you know, and encouragement to do what makes me happy.